BUILDING BLOCKS

BUILDING BLOCKS

Stories of Neighborhood
Transformation From
Strong City Baltimore

First Edition

ISBN: 978-1-62720-271-8

Printed in the United States of America

Published by Apprentice House Press

Apprentice House Press
Loyola University Maryland
4501 N. Charles Street
Baltimore, MD 21210
410.617.5265
www.ApprenticeHouse.com
info@ApprenticeHouse.com

Contents

ACKNOWLEDGEMENTS

Creating these narratives would not have been possible without the generous support of the Fund for Change, which provided the seed funding for Strong City Baltimore to take the time to conduct the requisite research and write up the extensive history of our work with these neighborhoods.

We owe special thanks to the "community readers" and friends of Strong City who pored over these accounts, checking them for accuracy and suggesting helpful changes. Readers who contributed edits and comments include Paul Brophy, Joann Levy, Kate Lynch, Joseph B. McNeely, Bill Miller, Erin O'Keefe, Salem Reiner, Connie Ross, Lottie Sneed, Catherine Stokes, and city Department of Housing and Community Development leaders Michael Braverman, Stacy Freed, Jason Hessler, and Jim Majors. Thanks, also, to our longstanding partner Loyola University Maryland and its Apprentice House Press. Tamara Payne, in addition to being one of our readers, is the force behind the Barclay School mosaic pictured on our cover, which she created in collaboration with community members.

We would be remiss not to thank the people of Remington, Harwood, Barclay, and the York Road neighborhoods, especially those who agreed to be interviewed and quoted for this project. Their aspirations, struggles, strengths, challenges – their very lives – are documented in these pages, and these stories are theirs as much as ours.

Finally, we acknowledge the invaluable contributions of former Strong City Executive Directors Dick Cook, Bill Miller, and Sandy Sparks, along with the many dozens of Strong City staff, AmeriCorps VISTA (Volunteers in Service to America) members, and others who supported neighborhood leaders in countless ways over the past two decades.

In typical Strong City fashion, this book was a collaboration, created by many contributors over several years. The following members of the Strong City research and writing team were integral to its completion:

Writer and Lead Editor: Mike Cross-Barnet
Editor: Karen D. Stokes
Editor: Karen DeCamp
Writer and Editor: Josh Clement
Writer and Researcher: Christy Zuccarini
Photos: Mike Cross-Barnet, Samantha Solomon, and the Strong City archives

FOREWORD

The communities you are about to meet and the accounts of years of collaboration between Strong City Baltimore and the people who live and work there reveal in detail the crucial importance of long-term, thoughtful planning and ground-level organizing in neighborhood development. As important, they illustrate the reality of just how long it takes to restore a community and improve its future prospects.

The business of restoring cities requires taking the long view. It is not for those who lack patience or energy. That, as much as anything, is the lesson of these stories.

Truth be told, I have had a long professional and personal connection with Strong City, including having lived inside its original geographic boundaries for nearly 30 years. And so I am very well acquainted with the need to bring to the work an appreciation of a long time horizon.

Building, and then sustaining, Strong City and organizations like it requires early, dependable and patient investment in the vision of what is possible and the organizational structure and staff capacity to get there. That is why the Goldseker Foundation, both during and after my time there, committed significant funding to support both Strong City's programming and its internal operations. Both are necessary for success.

As it enters its sixth decade, Strong City presents in these pages a clear sense of its history, its identity, its accomplishments, and its aspirations – for itself and for the city it serves.

> — Timothy D. Armbruster, Former President, Goldseker Foundation and Baltimore Community Foundation

"The business of restoring cities requires taking the long view. It is not for those who lack patience or energy."
– *former Goldseker Foundation President Timothy D. Armbruster*

EXECUTIVE SUMMARY

This document presents a series of narratives showing how Strong City Baltimore, a grassroots nonprofit based in Baltimore City since 1969, has put its community building principles into action in three distinct neighborhoods – Remington, Harwood, and Barclay – as well as a coalition of north-central neighborhoods, the York Road Partnership. (Strong City has worked in other communities, but this project focuses only on these areas.)

When Strong City is invited to work in a community, its preferred model is to send paid community organizers who engage with residents and anchor institutions to map assets, identify stakeholders, connect people to resources, and build leadership capacity. Our *place-based strategy* is holistic, building on existing strengths and embracing all the elements of a community that must be healthy for it to thrive: schools, businesses, housing, recreation, neighborhood leadership, and more. These four case studies document how this approach, applied consistently over an extended period, can yield significant positive results.

In Barclay, Strong City provided a wide range of supportive services in our role as community advocate and intermediary between neighborhood residents and a socially responsible developer charged with creating mixed-income housing and community spaces. In Harwood, we took a truly holistic approach: facilitating block projects, training resident leaders, strengthening the local school, supporting youth in need of positive activities, and stepping in to operate an abandoned recreation center.

In Remington, we supported the formation of a new, energetic neighborhood association that sought to revive a sense of civic purpose, and we also worked with a community-minded builder who revived a vacant warehouse and created needed housing. On York Road, in collaboration with Loyola University Maryland, we nurtured a coalition of neighborhoods that has worked hard to bridge one of Baltimore's toughest racial and class divides, coming together to address problems of concern to all.

In each of these cases, Strong City played a vigorous but supporting role – always working toward goals set by residents themselves, never presuming to "fix" a neighborhood or to impose an outsider's view of what should be done.

We have learned, and are now sharing, a number of key lessons from this work, among them:

1. Although each neighborhood's strengths and challenges are unique, there are common themes that can be transferred from place to place.

2. The role of trained community organizers in strengthening disinvested communities is critical and should be supported with philanthropic and government funding.

3. Community organizers help people establish group goals and strategies and take collective action to build power and make lasting impact.

4. Racial divisions and past and present structural racism need to be identified and addressed head-on.

5. Tangible, physical improvements – from planting a garden to painting a mural to rehabbing a vacant house – are indispensable to creating a sense of power and effectiveness.

6. Perhaps most crucially, we have learned that real, sustainable change is possible, but it requires *patience, persistence, and a commitment to collective action.*

The desire for fast and easy solutions is understandable. People want change in their communities *now* – not 10 years from now. But the hard truth is that there are no quick fixes to the problems of neglected urban neighborhoods in Baltimore (or, we believe, anywhere else). It took decades of disinvestment for these places to become distressed; no surprise, then, that it has taken a decade or more of concerted effort to make significant progress toward turning things around.

INTRODUCTION

Who We Are

Established in 1969, Strong City Baltimore is a grassroots nonprofit organization whose mission is to build and strengthen neighborhoods and people across Baltimore City, and beyond. We enhance the capacity of residents and social change-makers to improve their communities. Strong City believes Baltimore is made stronger through the work of community-based initiatives and leaders.

We began as Greater Homewood Community Corporation – an organization born in the aftermath of the 1968 civil unrest and devoted to community development in north-central Baltimore. Our goal was to strengthen city neighborhoods in response to growing middle-class white and black flight. Over the past half-century, we have forged many successful partnerships and coalitions, expanding the services we provide and the geographic area we influence.

Our work is based on a model of community building that includes identifying and strengthening neighborhood assets and addressing challenges: increasing the number of engaged residents, developing community leaders, remediating blighted and vacant properties, bolstering schools, promoting investment and homeownership, and advocating for policies and funding that improve the quality of life. Supporting community-driven initiatives through fiscal sponsorship has become an important tool for carrying out our mission in recent years. Recognizing the historical and ongoing impact of institutional racism in Baltimore, we also seek to employ a lens of racial equity in our work.

At the dawn of the 2020s, Strong City's robust program of fiscal sponsorship, diverse direct-service initiatives, and annual Neighborhood Institute had been serving the whole city for years, and we had changed our name in 2015 to reflect this organizational evolution. After 50 years in north-central Baltimore, Strong City relocated in early 2020 to a renovated printing plant in an East Baltimore neighborhood challenged by disinvestment but brimming with possibility.

While we have always relied on the grassroots support of thousands of ordinary Baltimoreans, the backing of institutional funders such as Johns Hopkins University, Loyola University Maryland, and the Goldseker Foundation has been indispensable to success in the neighborhoods profiled here. Of special note, the Homewood Community Partners Initiative (HCPI), launched by Johns Hopkins in December 2012 and implemented in partnership with residents, business leaders, nonprofits, and government, directed $10 million over five years toward the estimated cost of $60 million to implement 29 community-driven recommendations in 10 neighborhoods. Some funding for the work Strong City did in Harwood, Barclay and Remington after 2012 was drawn from HCPI money.

Our successful work has also relied on deep ties with other nonprofits, including the Central Baltimore Partnership, whose 100-plus partners implement a comprehensive strategy for community revival in 11 Central Baltimore neighborhoods and one commercial district; and Healthy Neighborhoods, which helps strong but undervalued city neighborhoods increase home values, market their communities, create high standards for property improvements, and forge strong connections among neighbors.

Even as Strong City has grown and evolved, we remained bound to the core values upon which we were founded. We know that organized neighborhoods can tap into the energies and gifts of their residents to build collective power – power that can be used to build up assets, address problems, hold government accountable, and create great places to live. We also know that organized action is crucial to building strong communities.

> Even as Strong City has grown and evolved, we remained bound to the core values upon which we were founded.

A Place-Based Strategy

Grassroots organizing is the heart and soul of Strong City Baltimore's neighborhood work. Experience shows that the prerequisites for a successful neighborhood organizing effort include, at a minimum: 1) a competent, experienced sponsoring organization; 2) patient, reliable financial support (because results may not become evident for many years); and 3) a talent pool of trained organizers.

Strong City employs trained community organizers to connect residents and inspire people to action. Starting on the ground, we go door-to-door in neighborhoods where our assistance is desired, meeting neighbors, listening, and building relationships. After identifying established and emerging local leaders, we may work with local anchors to facilitate the creation of a block network and a plan to build the capacity of the community association. Together, we plan and implement block captain trainings and other leadership development programming. New leaders are encouraged to take on projects and get involved in larger community issues.

While helping to form a stronger block network within the community, we also work to connect the neighborhood to larger efforts and institutions, such as local schools, elected officials, coalitions, universities, citywide advocacy groups, and more. We know that developing neighborhood capacity requires harnessing the energy of local people. This begins with hearing what people have to say and identifying collective issues, while working closely with stakeholders over time to develop practical solutions.

The stories presented here will show that successful community building depends in part on the presence of a paid organizer who builds the capacity of people and organizations to maximize power. As the Western Organization of Resource Councils (WORC) states, "Organizers are responsible for expanding the membership base [of community groups], maintaining a focus on action, and preserving democratic, participatory structures and processes."[I]

An organizer's role is to mobilize people in a community and help them understand the issues that are impeding progress. Organizers listen to those who know the community, and begin by meeting people where they are. They recruit and develop leaders. They convene, in WORC's words, "a diverse group ... who agree to serve as their community's public voice on a variety of issues."[II]

Organizers are responsible for sharing information and presenting questions, options, alternatives, and problems that affect the collective power the group can wield. Organizers do their fair share of the work, while also striving never to do for others what they can do for themselves. In other words, organizers work *with, not for*, their constituents.

Organizers engage with local people to define problems and strengths and help them think through strategies and tactics necessary to act with confidence and achieve community goals. With on-the-ground community organizing that connects directly and deeply with residents, efforts to address persistent problems facing neighborhoods are much more likely to succeed.

In contrast to the organizing style of advocacy

groups that focus on a single issue or take explicit political stances, Strong City employs a *place-based strategy* – a flexible model that can adapt to locations, needs and issues, developing organically to create sustainable community change. Critical to our approach is the assumption, borrowed from the model of Asset-Based Community Development (ABCD), that even the most challenged neighborhoods have resources: passionate people with skills, knowledge, and commitment; strong relationships; and key institutions.

These are the major components of Strong City's community building model:

1. **Always start with people.** Identify residents who want to make a change. They are the community's future leaders, though they might not know it yet.

2. **Map the assets.** Early work involves engaging resources and institutions that could have a positive impact over time, including: civic organizations, relevant city agencies, elected officials, schools, businesses, nonprofits and anchor institutions such as universities and places of worship. A place-based strategy builds on these existing assets.

3. **Address vacant and blighted properties** by working with residents to identify the worst properties and using a strategic approach that partners with the city Department of Housing & Community Development (DHCD) to result in demolition or renovation and new in-

vestment, depending on the market strengths of the block or neighborhood.

4. **Strengthen under-resourced public schools** by engaging the principal, families, teachers, students, and surrounding residents and businesses to reimagine schools as neighborhood hubs of resources and opportunities. This work includes empowering parents to advocate for their children.

5. **Create visible change** through block and greening projects that connect people and build on a sense of pride and care in their homes and neighborhoods.

6. **Promote economic development** by partnering with local institutions and businesses to encourage developing underutilized properties and providing access to goods and services the community wants and needs.

7. **Connect residents to opportunities** for home-ownership and wealth building.

Critical to our approach is the assumption that even the most challenged neighborhoods have resources: passionate people with skills, knowledge, and commitment; strong relationships; and key institutions.

The Stages of Neighborhood Organizing

In each of these narratives, just a handful of pages describes an arc of time covering many years, sometimes decades. This is not an attempt to tell the "whole" story of how these places have changed (if such a thing is even possible). Nor do these accounts fully convey the stop and start, two-steps-forward-one-step-back nature of these efforts. Progress toward neighborhood transformation does not proceed in a straight line, and anyone attempting this work should understand that delays, setbacks, and frustration come with the territory.

In the words of Joseph B. McNeely, former longtime Executive Director of the Central Baltimore Partnership (CBP) and a community organizer for 50 years: "Don't be discouraged – if you're doing the right thing, it *will* go off the rails from time to time. This is not about not making mistakes; this is about how you recover from your mistakes."

Strong City's model of organizing generally unfolds in the following sequence:

1. **Finding the insertion point.** This is the way an organizer enters a community, which ideally will connect to delivering something residents need. For Strong City, our insertion point is most often programmatic: operating a community school or a recreation center, for example. There may be multiple insertion points occurring at different times.

2. **Quick success to establish credibility.** Iron-

ically, although transformative community change takes a decade or more, no progress is possible without an early accomplishment or two to win buy-in from residents. This can be quite small: getting streetlights fixed, planting a community garden, organizing a school backpack giveaway.

3. **Relationship building**. The first two stages lead to growing trust and acceptance of the organizer by community members. Real relationships begin to form, based on mutual respect and affection.

4. **The "Aha!" moment.** After relationships are established and trust develops, the organizer and residents will be able to clarify the challenge or issue facing the community and figure out what needs to be done to get the neighborhood "unstuck" and allow progress to occur.

Purpose of These Stories

Strong City has a half-century of experience partnering with residents to bring about the changes they desire for their communities. And yet, until now, our methods, lessons, and successes have never been written down in an easily shareable way, so that others may benefit from this history. This book is an effort to do exactly that. The changes on view in places such as Barclay and Remington may seem obvious to casual observers, but the backstory is largely invisible. We are pulling back the curtain to reveal what happens behind the scenes of neighborhood transformation.

Each of the following stories illustrates the key components for a successful community-change initiative. They also reveal how each initiative is unique and nimble, bringing in a variety of partners (not necessarily always the same ones) that are critical to a neighborhood achieving its goals. As these cases demonstrate, creating lasting community change takes time. The work that was done in the communities profiled here spanned many years, with the core group sometimes changing its makeup but continually informed by community-articulated goals.

Each of the four cases documented here also demonstrates the kind of relationships that Strong City has built to address complex local challenges. In each instance, the success that was realized depended on the key ingredients of *trust* – the faith that partners will honor their commitments, no matter how difficult the work – and *assets*, those sometimes-hidden strengths all communities possess. These are, in the words of our book title, the "building blocks" of collective power; once that power is built and harnessed, change can take place.

Strong City Baltimore's work has been accelerated by collaboration with anchors in each community. This work, in part, focuses on promoting the community development model that our experience has shown to be so powerful.

These success stories constitute narrative content, program models, and indicative data to share in our community building efforts. They present a replicable model that others in the Baltimore metro area and other places (especially older, post-industrial cities) may find useful. They are also a signal to wary funders that, to echo Tim Armbruster in his Foreword, neighborhood organizing is worth the investment. Finally, we believe they are simply good stories – carefully documented, sometimes surprising, full of challenge, hope, and humanity. We expect that many readers will benefit from what we have learned.

A quick word about our name: From its inception in 1969 until 2015, the organization chronicled in these pages was called Greater Homewood Community Corporation (GHCC). Greater Homewood is the name by which we were known for the vast majority of the period covered here. For simplicity's sake, this book generally dispenses with our former name and uses "Strong City Baltimore" or "Strong City" throughout.

BARCLAY

Background

Barclay is a small, centrally located neighborhood near Amtrak's Penn Station and the Jones Falls Expressway. Its borders are North Avenue on the south, 25th Street on the north, Greenmount Avenue on the east and Calvert Street on the west. Its history reaches back over 200 years to a time when the area was peppered with country estates and served as a retreat for wealthy merchants and manufacturers.

With the completion of bridges across the Jones Falls after the Civil War, the area began quickly urbanizing. By the mid-1870s, Barclay and surrounding areas were being rapidly developed and continued to grow in population well into the early 1900s. By 1906, electric streetcars ran along all major roads, creating a huge suburban development boom that continued into the 1940s, when many middle-class and working-class white residents left the city to buy homes in the surrounding counties.

Public housing programs were implemented as part of the New Deal, and by the 1950s nearly 7,000 segregated public units had been built throughout Baltimore City, including in Barclay. Additionally, as houses started to go vacant in the 1960s and 1970s, the Housing Authority of Baltimore City (HABC) started buying up low-cost homes for scattered-site public housing.

From the middle of the century onward, Baltimore's white population continued to decline while its black population grew. Communities such as Barclay suffered from subpar housing, high rates of infant mortality, and significantly more crime than white communities. They also suffered disproportionately from the decline in Baltimore's manufacturing sector. Black unemployment was more than double the national rate, and even higher in especially poor communities. Those who did have jobs were paid less and often worked in unsafe conditions.

By 2000, Barclay was experiencing a huge increase in vacant houses. Over the years, the city had become owner of a significant number of wholly or partially vacant buildings after two privately owned HUD-insured housing projects had failed, largely as a result of poor maintenance of the properties. Crime and drug activity were also at an all-time high due to an uptick of gang members migrating to Baltimore, attracted by the ease of running criminal enterprises out of a major city along the I-95 corridor. In response, the city installed blue-light crime cameras throughout the neighborhood for surveillance and to scare off offenders.

Approaching the Work

Strong City Baltimore's community building efforts in Barclay were initially small-scale and focused mainly on sanitation. "In the beginning, it is important to keep it simple," explained former Strong City Executive Director Bill Miller. "Most of our lower-income neighborhoods wanted to combat rats, and so we often organized around that issue. These same communities suffered from serious crime problems, but rats were a proxy for fighting crime in communities where residents were afraid to openly confront drug dealers and violent neighbors."

In the late 1990s, Strong City launched an organizing effort around the formation of block clubs. At the time, AmeriCorps VISTA members carried out most of Strong City's organizing work, engaging with residents on specific blocks to organize projects and activities that would improve quality of life. These residents walked their streets and led over a dozen block projects that were funded in large part by the Baltimore Community Foundation. By 1999, Strong City had established a network of 16 block clubs, which eventually evolved into the Barclay Leadership Council (BLC), chaired by Helen Holmes and then Mary McPhail. In a 1999 article in *The Afro-American*, the BLC was described as "the fruit of [Strong City's] organizing effort."[III]

With guidance and technical support from Strong City, the BLC developed a strategy to eliminate sanitation problems by coordinating an annual neighborhood-wide cleanup called Helping Hands Day. Volunteers and neighborhood residents worked side by side to clean their streets, while the city provided tools and trucks. Additional funding support was provided by the Lutheran Brotherhood (currently called Thrivent Financial).

One of the BLC's most notable projects was the transformation of an inner-block vacant lot into a multi-use community garden. The project, done in partnership with the Parks & People Foundation's (PPF) Vacant Lot and Restoration Program, gained the BLC recognition throughout the community, and in 2000, they were given the Hathaway Ferebee Neighborhood Achievement Award for their work.[IV]

Over the next two years, the BLC transformed three more vacant lots into green spaces and gardens with PPF funding.[V]

What would prove to be a turning point for Barclay came in 2002, when then-Baltimore Mayor Martin O'Malley launched Project 5,000, which set out to acquire and return 5,000 vacant and abandoned properties to productive use. At the time, the vacancy rate in Baltimore was among the highest in the U.S. at 14.1 percent.[VI]

In Barclay, which was among the 10 main neighborhoods targeted by Project 5,000, the vacancy rate was nearly 40 percent.[VII]

Barclay residents – many of them already members of the BLC – approached Strong City for assistance with organizing around the impending redevelopment of their neighborhood. Strong City's strategy was to help develop a body of resident leaders and local stakeholders through which the community could engage developers and city entities to ensure that their concerns were addressed.

> "In the beginning, it is important to keep it simple."
> – *Bill Miller, former Strong City Executive Director*

From Vision to Action

After Mayor O'Malley announced the launch of Project 5,000, Strong City assisted with the formation of the Barclay Midway Old Goucher Coalition (BMOG), which was launched in summer 2003, with longtime residents Connie Ross and Jennifer Martin serving as co-chairs. "For two years, we talked about what we wanted and didn't want in the area," Ms. Connie recalled. "We worked on a plan, had a lot of meetings, charrettes, and workshops where everybody was able to express what they thought would make Barclay a whole lot better than it was. There were so many dilapidated and empty buildings, unused lots. The city really was our biggest landlord in the area, and they were not doing anything with their properties."

In the spring of 2005, the HABC released a Request for Qualifications (RFQ) for the redevelopment of properties in Barclay. In January 2006, city housing officials and the community selected Telesis Corporation, a mission-driven real estate development company based in Washington, D.C., to lead the revitalization of Barclay and its neighboring community Old Goucher.

Telesis, which worked hand in hand with the BMOG Coalition, developed a plan to transform Barclay into a stable, mixed-income neighborhood with quality open spaces, community facilities, and employment opportunities. "That's been a good relationship," Connie Ross said of Telesis. "They came in, and for a year and a half talked to every organization and every entity that had anything to do with the project, to get everyone's input." This included Michael Mazepink and Sandra Coles with People's Homesteading Group, a local developer.

Because Strong City had established itself as a reputable organization through its prior organizing efforts in Barclay, BMOG and Telesis chose it to serve as the primary service provider for this unprecedented redevelopment project. Connie Ross identifies Bill Miller as one of the key people advocating early on for the city to invest in Barclay, a partnership that would continue and grow under CEO Karen D. Stokes and Community Revitalization Coordinator Peter Duvall.

Strong City was the partner Barclay residents trusted to hold the developers accountable for ensuring the plan satisfied their priorities: a mixed-income, racially diverse community welcoming of both renters and homeowners, and preserving much of the historic architecture of the neighborhood.

"They worked with us from the very beginning," Ms. Connie says of Strong City. "They have just been with us through everything we've gone through – we've built a lot of great relationships with people at [Strong

City], and their input helped us to establish what we have now."

At a 2004 press conference on Project 5,000, then-Housing Commissioner Paul T. Graziano jokingly stated, "We've got all kinds of property. You want 'em, we got 'em!"[VIII] Finding buyers was integral to the project's intent to serve as a tool for rebuilding neighborhoods rather than simply eliminating blight.

The BMOG Coalition sent an open letter to Commissioner Graziano demanding "a seat at any table" where decisions about their future were to be made. They were concerned that the scope of the project was too focused on housing, thereby neglecting commercial districts, neighborhood infrastructure, and overall quality of life. BMOG also wanted to ensure that development moved toward a more even distribution of subsidized housing, to avoid repeating the historic pattern of concentrating low-income residents on certain blocks.

In 2005, at the same time that BMOG was negotiating with the Housing Authority, they were also at odds with the city over the state parole and probation building (2100 Guilford) located across the street from the Dallas F. Nicholas Sr. Elementary School. Dallas Nicholas Principal Irma Johnson contacted Strong City for assistance with advocating for moving the facility out of this residential neighborhood. At the time, hundreds of people were reporting daily to their parole or probation officer at the site, and for many, drug testing was required. The school, parents and community members became alarmed when stories surfaced that children were being offered money for clean urine samples. Removal of the facility became a priority for Strong City and BMOG. Over the years, there was a steady drumbeat of advocacy to local and state government officials to close the site.

In October 2006, Telesis hosted a design workshop at Dallas Nicholas, where residents provided feedback on conceptual alternatives for development in Barclay. The result was a formalized plan calling for the redevelopment of 268 properties. These included 102 scattered-site public housing units, 30 city-owned vacant lots, 77 vacant and abandoned properties, and a 91-unit Section 8 property.

Telesis submitted its plan, which was guided by a series of community goals set forth by the BMOG Coalition, to city housing officials in 2007, when Jennifer Martin, co-chair of BMOG, was replaced by Devon Wilford-Said. As the primary service provider for the redevelopment project, Strong City's designated role was to help ensure that these community goals were met.

In the midst of these redevelopment efforts, Barclay was grappling with an upsurge in violence and homicides. Mothers in the neighborhood came to Strong City seeking help with Barclay's middle school boys – too old for church-run summer camps and too young for the city's YouthWorks job program – who needed a positive summertime activity that would enrich them and keep them out of harm's way. Strong City responded by working with the community to design the Barclay Boys Summer Rites Program, an eight-week day camp that engaged 10 boys in challenging academics, field trips, and outdoor activities.

This program recruited boys with a family member who had been killed, or who were vulnerable to joining a gang. The camp was designed to offer an alternative rites-of-passage experience, utilizing a system based on African rituals. This was important, as it offered a positive challenge for the boys as an alternative to a gang's initiation rituals. The youths were also taken on camping trips and tested on teamwork and commitment to achievable goals.

Waiting for traditional foundation grant cycles was not possible in this case, because there was an urgent need for the program to launch by the summer. Strong City raised the needed funds through the Greater Homewood Interfaith Alliance – a group of churches and individuals along the North Charles Street corridor. Led by longtime Barclay resident and Dallas Nicholas Community School Coordinator Nate Tatum (now deceased), the Barclay Boys played chess and tennis, visited museums, scrubbed stoops for neighbors, and learned martial arts. The program paid each participant a stipend that many contributed to their families' income. Program leaders and neighborhood elders assigned to each Barclay Boy also provided strong African-American male role models. By the end of the summer, all 10 Barclay Boys had successfully completed the program, which continued each summer for the next several years.

Telesis' proposed project would unfold in four stages at a total cost of $85 million, including tens of millions in federal and city support. They anticipated that funding would come primarily from a combination of state and city contributions, requiring Low-Income Housing Tax Credit equity and Rental Housing Program loans.

With neighborhood outreach support from Strong City VISTAs, the BMOG Coalition and Telesis continued to host community meetings to discuss ongoing resident needs. In December 2008, Telesis and Strong City signed a Memorandum of Understanding (MOU) around the hiring of additional organizing staff to ensure that any identified service gaps in the community could be filled.

It took until July 2009 to secure the public financing Telesis needed to begin Phase 1A, which focused on rehabilitation and new construction of affordable housing rental units. Strong City hired two part-time organizers and renewed its contract for a VISTA dedicated to Barclay. Telesis provided neighborhood-based office space for all three staff, who would focus on helping to ensure an equitable and participatory community development process. In the months that followed, Strong City established a number of partnerships with key stakeholders to begin implementing the community's redevelopment agenda. Telesis broke ground on Phase 1A in September 2010.

In February 2011, Strong City secured a grant to establish and operate the Barclay Youth Safe Haven, which provided after-school homework assistance, social support, one-on-one mentoring, nutrition, and youth advocacy by specially trained police and civilian staff. Funding came from the Eisenhower Foundation, and just over 50 students at Dallas Nicholas enrolled. (As a Title I school, Dallas Nicholas served large numbers of students and families in poverty. Additionally, it was challenged by chronic absenteeism and low parent involvement.)

Prior to the Safe Haven initiative, Strong City had served Dallas Nicholas for the past decade, previously sponsoring an AmeriCorps VISTA to organize parents and offer after-school programs to students. With Barclay Youth Safe Haven in place, Strong City was able to bring positive and mutually beneficial change to the school and its community.

In December 2011, Telesis agreed to fund a full-time Community Builder through Strong City to oversee all organizing activity in Barclay. Based on the feedback collected at earlier community meetings, a Resident Services Plan had been developed, with the recommendation to provide outreach services to the community. With full-time, on-the-ground staff in place, Strong City had essentially doubled its capacity to provide such services, including in the areas of youth development, community building, job training and job opportunities.

Building on those efforts, Strong City in 2012 began offering career development services aimed at better preparing adults to enter and stay in the workforce. Utilizing a one-year funding commitment from the Baltimore Integration Partnership (BIP) via the Central Baltimore Partnership (CBP), Strong City implemented a pilot program of workforce pipeline services for low-income/low-skilled residents in Barclay.

One year later, with funding from the CBP via a Baltimore Regional Neighborhood Initiative (BRNI) grant, Strong City hired a full-time Workforce Transition Coordinator, providing the staff capacity to manage this pipeline efficiently. Strong City's career development services, coupled with its community organizing efforts, were guided by the priorities Barclay had set for itself.

Also in 2013, after a series of relational one-on-one meetings, door-to-door campaigns, and small group meetings, issues were prioritized and addressed. The top priorities were blight removal, cleaning and greening of public spaces, and positive youth engagement. In 2014, a collaborative of Barclay leaders supported by Lottie Sneed, then Strong City's Barclay Community Builder, secured funding from the CBP's Johns Hopkins University-funded Community Spruce-Up Grant program to launch the "Bold, Beautiful and Brilliant Barclay" initiative. The initiative improved the aesthetics and ambiance of the neighborhood by cleaning and transforming unattended lots with foliage and gardens, using art to bring new life to vacant buildings, planting trees, addressing illegal dumping and litter through education, leading regular cleanups, and installing trash receptacles along heavily used pedestrian routes.

The following year, organizing efforts focused on youth development. Ms. Lottie and residents held gatherings in the local park, and, based on conversations with youth, initiated a series of summer youth clubs. Through partnerships and small grants, Ms. Lottie and resident leaders held bike repair workshops, and organized community bike rides and introductions to architecture and business via on-site clubs. The community came together for what became an annual cookout and movie night in the park.

To address the needs of young adult mothers, Ms. Lottie partnered with another local nonprofit to host an annual women's empowerment conference. All of the work started through a visible presence in the community, first winning trust and then moving into positive intervention.

According to Ms. Lottie, "the beauty of the work is that it is vibrant and dynamic. You can never grow weary of the surprise and joy of meeting new people and realizing that together, great things can be accomplished." That respect for consistent and persistent engagement brought many community partners to the table, including BMOG, local schools and churches, the CBP, the City of Baltimore, community associations, and youth and adult resident leaders.

Over the years since "Bold, Beautiful, and Brilliant Barclay" was launched, there has been a healthy infusion of new homeowners and renters – brought in by the continued expansion and evolution of the redevelopment by Telesis. So the next focus was on training these new leaders to create strong block networks, with a specific eye toward youth development and young adult activities.

Ms. Lottie continued to use door-to-door outreach to determine the needs of residents and to promote communal activities and participation, and to connect residents with city services and other resources. The work she started was continued by Farajii Muhammad, who succeeded her as Barclay Community Builder from 2017 until 2019, when Telesis brought its community engagement work in-house.

> "They worked with us from the very beginning. We've built a lot of great relationships with people at [Strong City], and their input helped us to establish what we have now."
>
> – Connie Ross, Barclay community leader

Where We Are and Where We're Going

Around the city, advocates including Strong City have pointed out problems with the city's weak inclusionary housing law and are pushing for developers to include more units for low-income residents. But in Barclay, 200 affordable homes for low- and moderate-income households were added during the 2010s. This has been accomplished through partnership among neighborhood residents, Telesis, and Strong City, with crucial support from the city, state, and HABC, which provided significant land and funding.

An additional 100 affordable and market-rate homes and 10,000 square feet of community and retail space were either under construction or in the immediate pipeline in late 2019. Telesis also renovated and now manages the Rental Assistance Demonstration

(RAD) project, a 150-unit high rise nearby on 25th Street. According to Catherine Stokes, Vice President/ Director of Telesis Baltimore, at the close of 2019 the company's work in Barclay was 75 percent complete.

With the Telesis redevelopment chugging along, Barclay (and Harwood) received more good news in 2015 when Baltimore City launched the LINCS program (Leveraging Investments in Neighborhood Corridors) to revitalize some of the city's most important traffic corridors, starting with Greenmount Avenue, a long-neglected north-south artery. This action, and the city's prioritization of the Greenmount Corridor, followed advocacy by Strong City and BMOG. Because of Strong City's long history of involvement with the Greenmount neighborhoods, it was selected as the lead engagement partner, ensuring that community voices would be heard and that the city agencies implementing LINCS would respond to local needs.

The Urban Land Institute issued a comprehensive report with goals relating to safety, revitalization, transit, and other priorities. Progress on LINCS has been slow but steady; among the more visible improvements are the beautiful new façade of the Greenmount Recreation Center and a new crosswalk designed to protect youths transiting between the rec center and Mund Park across the street. Other changes include traffic signal prioritization for buses; various traffic calming interventions; and increased code enforcement. As of late 2019, Baltimore and Strong City were continuing to partner on the LINCS program.

Strong City also became increasingly active with code enforcement efforts in Barclay. Thanks in large part to the work of Peter Duvall and his assistant, Rachel Shane, the number of vacant homes in Barclay had dropped to 92 as of late 2019, a reduction of more than 60 percent over a decade. Two dozen vacant houses were either under rehabilitation or slated for demolition, while several dozen others faced vacant building receivership suits.

As the decade closed out, even a long-elusive solution to the parole and probation saga was finally within reach. The building at 2100 Guilford Ave. was completely vacated in December 2019, and the state was accepting submissions for redevelopment of the site. BMOG and other community groups provided input on the kinds of new uses residents would find acceptable.

It had become clear that a once seemingly lost neighborhood had begun to achieve a significant turnaround, grounded in priorities identified by Barclay residents.

"For years, the chances of a Barclay comeback seemed bleak," wrote *Baltimore Sun* reporter Jacques Kelly in a 2013 article about the neighborhood.[IX]

But after chatting with a neighbor who was planning to move into a newly renovated Telesis home, Kelly recognized how much progress this promising neighborhood had made. "Many parties are now taking a stand here: concerned residents, developers, the city's housing department and others, including home buyers who want to live in an old Baltimore neighborhood," he wrote.

The catalyst for Barclay's resurgence harks back to 2005, with the creation of the Barclay-Midway-Old Goucher Small Area Plan – the community's first resident-led redevelopment vision and a direct result of intentional community organizing. After decades of disinvestment and decay, Barclay was clearly rebounding and had once again become a place where people wanted to live and where they could feel proud.

> "Many parties are now taking a stand here: concerned residents, developers, the city's housing department and others, including home buyers who want to live in an old Baltimore neighborhood."
> – *Jacques Kelly*, **Baltimore Sun**

Key Strategies: Barclay

1. **Mixed-Income Community**. With the support of Strong City, the Barclay Midway Old Goucher Coalition (BMOG) made clear that it wanted a mix of public, low- and moderate-income, and market-rate housing. The Telesis plan was created to meet that goal. With all-new, energy-efficient rehabs inside historic rowhomes and marketing help from Strong City, market-rate homes have sold in

the upper-$200,000s.

2. **Community Building**. While Telesis was building and renovating houses, Strong City focused on building community. Strong City used social events and activities as vehicles for interaction between new and old residents, including quarterly block parties, walking tours, cleanups, community gardens, a neighborhood newsletter, and continued block captain trainings.

3. **Social Services**. Strong City conducted outreach to new move-ins and existing residents, connecting them to supportive services and community resources. Particular attention was paid to residents with housing issues, with staff working to ensure that residents knew their rights as tenants and monitoring tenants who required special attention.

4. **Education and Youth Development**. Strong City worked to provide access to programs and resources for educational success and growth at all age levels, including support for neighborhood children in middle and high school, and adults seeking educational opportunities. Strong City also continued its partnership with Dallas F. Nicholas, Sr. Elementary School, which had potential to become an anchor for the community that attracted families to Barclay.

5. **Employment.** To increase employment opportunities for Barclay residents, Strong City, with the Central Baltimore Partnership, developed a Workforce Program that provided barrier-removal opportunities and job training skills.

Barclay Timeline/Fact Sheet

- In the 1990s, Strong City's AmeriCorps VISTAs help to form block clubs in Barclay, establishing a network of 16 of them by 1999 that evolve into the Barclay Leadership Council (BLC)
- Strong City organizers support BLC with sanitation, neighborhood cleanup projects
- In 2002, after the city names Barclay as one of 10 distressed communities targeted for revitalization, residents ask Strong City for help with the impending redevelopment
- In 2003, Strong City spearheads the creation of the Barclay Midway Old Goucher Coalition (BMOG) to give the community a voice in dealing with the city and developers
- In 2006, lead developer Telesis Corp. and the community select Strong City as the primary service provider for the Barclay redevelopment project; Strong City's role includes assuring the community's goals are met
- Strong City organizes block parties, walking

tours, cleanups, community gardens, a news-letter, and block captain trainings, and also helps residents with housing issues, connecting them to resources and tenant information

- Strong City becomes Community School administrator for Dallas F. Nicholas Sr. Elementary School and brings in a Coordinator to organize parents, provide after-school opportunities
- Strong City advocates with residents for removal of the problematic parole and probation building on Guilford Avenue
- In the late 2000s, Strong City and the community develop the Barclay Boys Summer Rites Program for middle-school boys who have faced trauma; all 10 boys enrolled complete the program, which continues for several years
- In 2009, Strong City hires additional staff dedicated to organizing in Barclay
- In 2011, Strong City launches the Barclay Youth Safe Haven program at Dallas Nicholas school
- In 2011, Strong City hires a full-time Community Builder for Barclay
- In 2012, in partnership with Central Baltimore Partnership (CBP) and Baltimore Integration Partnership (BIP), Strong City begins offering career development services for

Barclay residents, and later hires a Workplace Transition Coordinator

- Starting in 2014, the Barclay Community Builder launches a major greening initiative, followed by intensive youth development efforts including clubs for youth, cookouts, movie nights, a walking club, and a Women's Retreat
- Strong City's and BMOG's advocacy results in the addition of 200 low- and moderate-income housing units, with another 100 in the pipeline
- Thanks in large measure to Strong City's code enforcement work, vacancies in Barclay drop to fewer than 100, a reduction of more than 60% over a decade

With Strong City's support, Barclay leaders secured funding from Johns Hopkins through the Central Baltimore Partnership to launch the "Bold, Beautiful, and Brilliant Barclay" initiative. The project included transforming unattended lots with foliage and gardens.

In response to advocacy by Strong City and the Barclay-Midway-Old Goucher Coalition, Baltimore in 2015 launched the LINCS program to revitalize key city traffic corridors, starting with Greenmount Avenue. Strong City was named the lead engagement partner for LINCS.

Telesis-developed homes at the corner of Barclay and 20th streets. By the end of 2019, 200 homes for low- and moderate-income households had been added in Barclay, with another 100 affordable and market-rate homes under construction or in the immediate pipeline.

Strong City manages community improvement grants from Healthy Neighborhoods, Inc. on behalf of communities. An example is the Greenmount Rec Center, where artist Andy Dahl and Telesis worked with the community to transform the facility's façade and grounds.

HARWOOD

Background

Nestled in the heart of north-central Baltimore, Harwood encompasses about 14 city blocks. In the 1890s, the B&O Railroad constructed the Baltimore Belt Line through the neighborhood. Once the main passenger rail line into Baltimore from Philadelphia and New York, it evolved into a major freight route, with several trains passing through each day. Harwood was also home to Baltimore's early professional baseball teams, with the original Oriole Park once located in the north end of the neighborhood.

Most homes in Harwood are brick rowhouses built between 1900 and 1920. Harwood's population declined steadily in the latter half of the 20th century and early 21st century due to middle-class flight, petty crime, drug dealing, drug abuse, and other social ills. Harwood was still a majority white neighborhood into the 1970s but at the close of the 2010s was overwhelmingly African-American (with signs of increasing diversification in recent years).

In the late 1960s, Johns Hopkins University became involved in supporting the local Barclay Elementary/Middle School with members of the Hopkins Women's

Club and university faculty volunteering regularly. (Confusingly, the Barclay School is located in the Harwood neighborhood on Barclay Street – not in the nearby Barclay neighborhood.)

Esther Bonnet, who later became President of Strong City's Board of Directors, ran the Barclay School library. Strong City Baltimore inherited these ties when it was formed in 1969, and by the early 1970s Strong City AmeriCorps VISTA members were deployed at the school. Gertrude Williams, a visionary education leader who began as assistant principal in 1969, was promoted to principal in 1973. Under her leadership, community engagement grew exponentially.

Despite the strength of the Barclay School, the ensuing decades saw a period of steady neighborhood decline and disinvestment, and increasing crime. In winter 2005, things came to a head. Open-air drug markets had long thrived in the neighborhood, where local drug dealers controlled blocks filled with vacant and blighted homes.

Edna McAbier, who purchased her home in 1983, was an active resident and member of the Harwood Community Association. In 2002, Strong City's then-Executive Director Bill Miller encouraged Ms. McAbier to serve as the community association president. She ran and was elected. In this role, Ms. McAbier quickly became one of Harwood's greatest champions, known for telling drug dealers, "I don't want you on this corner."[X]

Many of Edna McAbier's neighbors trusted that she would get their complaints and concerns into the right hands, as she had formed a strong alliance with local police. But one early morning in January 2005, Ms. McAbier's home was firebombed with Molotov cocktails in retaliation. Eight people, including a prominent gang leader, were eventually arrested and sentenced to decades in prison. But Ms. McAbier, who had relocated into police protection, would never return to the neighborhood. Losing her was a hard hit for Harwood. The community association floundered as many residents simply stopped getting involved for fear of retaliation.

Approaching the Work

Improving public schools is a keystone of Strong City's community revitalization and neighborhood stabilization efforts because successful schools attract and retain families. For many years, Strong City VISTAs had been providing a great range of services to the Harwood neighborhood's Barclay School, where they worked to connect the school to program providers, funding sources, and volunteers, while also offering technical assistance and leadership development opportunities for parents and school staff.

Strong City worked in partnership with the Barclay School to establish an education committee of teachers, staff, parents, and residents. This committee evolved into its own independent group called the Barclay Brent Education Corporation (BBEC), which was dedicated to strengthening two local public schools – Barclay and Margaret Brent Elementary/Middle in Charles Village. Strong City and the Barclay School made extraordinary strides in curriculum development during Gertrude

Williams' tenure, which lasted until 1998. In the years that followed, Strong City maintained a presence in Harwood through its work at the school.

In 2005, Strong City applied for and received funding to implement a Community Schools model at the Barclay School, which would broaden the organization's reach in the school and neighborhood. By definition, a Community School is a network of partnerships between the school and other community resources that promote student achievement and family and community well-being. Its integrated focus on academics, enrichment, health and social supports, youth and community development, and family engagement leads to student success, strong families, and healthy communities. Partnerships allow schools to become resources to the community and offer programs and opportunities that are open to all.

In tandem with its work at the Barclay School, Strong City focused on attracting investment, providing resources to current residents, and building civic capacity. Harwood's high vacancy rate continued to cause challenges with regard to drug dealing and other crime, which put a strain on residents and deterred potential homebuyers and investors.

Baltimore's housing market typology had long classified Harwood as "Middle Market Stressed," meaning that it had considerable assets but also many "Distressed" blocks. Strong City had been providing grants for block projects through its Healthy Neighborhoods program for several years but would need to increase efforts around strategic code enforcement and marketing.

As in all of the neighborhoods where Strong City played a supportive role in building and promoting quality of life, attracting and retaining investment in Harwood was key to ensuring a successful turnaround. Issues with aging housing stock, vacancies, and crime presented challenges that required ongoing strategic efforts to improve the local public school, facilitate public and private investment, and encourage strong civic involvement by developing neighborhood leadership.

As in all of the neighborhoods where Strong City played a supportive role in building and promoting quality of life, attracting and retaining investment in Harwood was key to ensuring a successful turnaround.

From Vision to Action

In 2005, the year drug dealers firebombed Edna McAbier's home, Baltimore had begun to formally implement the national Community Schools model across the city, including at Barclay. With this model, schools became neighborhood hubs that brought educators, families, and community partners together to offer a range of opportunities, supports, and services to children, their families, and the community.

With funding from the Family League of Baltimore City, Strong City hired a full-time Community School Site Coordinator who worked alongside a full-time VISTA at the Barclay School. This increase in staff capacity enabled Strong City to ramp up its efforts and deepen its focus on tackling key issues in the school, as well as in the broader community: crime and drugs, and the lack of opportunities for youth, family support, and adult education.

Parent and family engagement was a key area of focus at the Barclay School, as Strong City was committed to developing parents as leaders. That meant forging relationships with parents and providing the kind of information, training, and technical assistance they needed to step into leadership roles. Organized groups were formed that included teachers, staff, parents, and community leaders who collaborated in making decisions that helped improve academic performance.

Additional outreach to parents and families included organizing well-attended family events that brought students' families into the schools and into contact with teachers. These events were designed to share information, provide resources and training for parents, and showcase student achievement.

Volunteer involvement was another integral component to building a successful Community School. Neighbors pitched in enthusiastically to support the school. One small group of neighbors planted and maintained gardens around the school and worked with student garden club members.

In concert with these efforts, Strong City staff cultivated relationships with local colleges and universities, businesses, and faith partners who, after being trained to fill in wherever support was needed, coordinated fundraisers, tutored students, staffed family events, and more. The Barclay School soon became a successful model of university-assisted programming, with staff and students from four local campuses regularly leading book clubs and after-school enrichment activities, tutoring, and aiding teachers.

By the 2009-2010 school year, Strong City's Barclay Community School Coordinator had built 28 active partnerships to meet student and family needs, enhance curriculum, and provide enrichment and support. Parent engagement was key to sustaining these efforts, and staff worked diligently to support strong parent-teacher organizations within the school and community. The Village Parents, which was launched by two neighborhood moms, collaborated closely with Strong City to help new neighborhood families become more acquainted with the school through tours and marketing efforts.

Also in 2009, Strong City secured funding from the Goldseker Foundation to launch a new marketing initiative it called Great Schools Charles Village, which supported both Barclay and Margaret Brent as key anchors for strengthening the community and attracting and retaining neighborhood families. Strong City vigorously reached out to the community with marketing materials and events, including a speaker series that was aimed at separating fact from myth about public schools.

With its own website and social media presence managed by Strong City staff and volunteers from Village Parents, Great Schools Charles Village promoted school and neighborhood activities, introduced new school staff, and shared helpful resources for families. Strong City also launched a campaign to raise funds for school improvement and foster collaboration and best-practice sharing between new young families and older neighbors who were involved with school-neighborhood organizing 30 years prior through the BBEC.

While community engagement at the Barclay School was thriving, involvement in the neighborhood at large was not as robust. In 2011, Strong City devised an organizing strategy with the goal of building participation in the Harwood Community Association and finding residents who would be excited to make visible improvements to their homes. Previous Healthy Neighborhoods block projects had been very successful in creating rowhome blocks with a unified, cared-for appearance, the best example being the 300 block of Lorraine Avenue with its glittering mosaic number plaques, mailboxes and flower boxes made by residents with the guidance of block resident and community artist Tamara Payne.

Tamara had moved to the neighborhood in 2007, and at first was taken aback by the trash in the streets and open drug dealing on the corners. But she also sensed the potential for change, and before long she was leaving her mark on the community. As she explained,

"I put a mosaic sign up on my house, and my neighbors said, 'Hey, where'd you get that from? It was a domino effect – neighbors started commissioning me for mosaics, year to year to year … and it grew until the whole block was done."

Building on the success Tamara's work inspired on Lorraine Avenue, Strong City conducted outreach to residents living on the 300 block of Ilchester Avenue – a designated Healthy Neighborhoods target block. Staff recruited 10 families to participate in the annual Charles Village Painted Ladies contest. Charles Village, a neighborhood just west of Harwood, had been running the contest since 1997 in an effort to encourage neighbors to spruce up the exterior of their homes with vibrant colors.

Strong City secured a grant from Healthy Neighborhoods to provide Harwood residents with paint and supplies, and each family participated for different reasons. In the essay that accompanied his before-and-after pictures, one resident noted that his grey house "didn't reflect the spirit of our block." He and his wife chose bright colors. Another family, who had lost two children in a fire 14 years earlier, said that the contest kept their spirits up. "We joined the neighbors to bring more life to this wonderful area in which we have lived for over 20 years," they wrote. All 10 families won first place in the Healthy Neighborhoods Initiative category. Harwood had something to be proud of.

In 2012, Strong City partnered with the University of Maryland School of Social Work Community Outreach Service (SWCOS) Neighborhood Fellows

Program to hire a School of Social Work graduate student to add staff capacity to its efforts in Harwood. Hannah Gardi remembers her first few weeks on the job. "I was working on the second annual Painted Ladies contest and walking around Harwood a lot. I started door knocking and getting to know people in the neighborhood," she said.

One day in October, Hannah received a phone call from a new, young homeowner in Harwood, Amanda Ruthven. Amanda explained that she was hosting a Halloween party for the neighborhood and asked if Strong City would help her distribute flyers. "Communication in Harwood was disjointed from block to block," explained Hannah. "We had no idea this event was even being planned."

Hannah joined Amanda in door knocking and distributing flyers, and Harwood Halloween, as it was called, ended up being instrumental in building cohesion among neighbors because, as Hannah put it, "it was completely spearheaded by them." Neighbors donated candy, and Amanda's future husband Ryan Parnell, who owned a construction company and a home in Harwood, transformed a vacant property into a haunted house. They also built a maze, and offered face painting and trick-or-treating at the nearby playground. People from all over the neighborhood attended. "It was a pivotal event," Hannah recalled.

But only a few months later, a new, unanticipated wave of violence swept through the neighborhood, leaving one 16-year-old dead and five people shot. A concerned community leapt into action, determined that history would not repeat itself in Harwood.

Strong City held a community meeting at its headquarters in Charles Village. New residents attended, as did old ones, who recalled the aftermath of what happened to Edna McAbier. Back then, "Everybody stopped. Everybody stopped going outside. Everybody stopped talking to each other. No one wanted to be seen as a leader," Hannah was told. But Harwood had come a long way since 2005, and the people who lived there were unwilling to step down. "This is our chance," said one resident. "Are we going to be afraid, stay in our house and close our doors, or are we going to do something?"

"Strong City gave people the courage to take ownership," Hannah said. In the following months, 16 Harwood residents, including Amanda Ruthven and Ryan Parnell, participated in a series of weekly block captain trainings and monthly Neighborhood Leaders Forums. Topics ranged from conflict management to community greening to fundraising. During all of the discussions, a recurring theme emerged: the need for new leadership in Harwood.

> "Strong City gave people the courage to take ownership."
> – Hannah Gardi, former Strong City organizer

The Harwood Community Association had been struggling to keep itself afloat for years, and its current president had expressed an interest in stepping down.

Amanda Ruthven was elected to take his place. "I want to be proud of my neighborhood," Amanda explained. "And since I bought a home here, I want that investment to pay off."

Despite residents' best efforts, pride and value can be hard to build in a neighborhood blighted by vacant houses. After the McAbier firebombing, longtime City Councilwoman Mary Pat Clarke had worked with the community association and Strong City to come up with a list of steps to improve the neighborhood. One critical step was to start putting vacants through the Vacant House Receivership process. Michael Braverman (later named the city's Housing Commissioner) was directing the department's Code Enforcement Legal Section at the time and asked for a list of 20 potential targets for prosecution.

As properties have been rehabilitated, more have been added to a community priority list that Strong City maintains and monitors. Peter Duvall, Strong City's Community Revitalization Coordinator, explains that individual attention to these properties is crucial, because bankruptcies and unusual title issues can make some houses immune from prosecution for years at a time.

For example, one of the original 20 houses, 348 E. 27th St., spent well over a decade in federal bankruptcy proceedings. The community and Strong City never gave up on turning this property around, viewing it as a top priority because the garage was collapsing onto the sidewalk. The collective efforts of the Legal Section, the community association, and Strong City were eventually rewarded when the property received a Use and Occupancy Permit in October 2018.

Complementing these efforts was an innovative approach to crime-fighting. In 2007, Baltimore Police Department (BPD) Officer Doug Gibson, a community-based officer in the Northern District, along with the Department of Housing & Community Development (DHCD) and other officials, worked with the community to identify problem residences that contributed to drug activity and crime. Gibson compiled incident reports while BPD executed search and seizure warrants that enabled DHCD's Code Enforcement attorneys to file drug nuisance cases. The property-based solution to drug nuisance in Harwood was highly successful and helped create an environment ripe for renovation and homeownership.

At four locations within Harwood, the seizures allowed Code Enforcement attorneys to file drug nuisance cases against the owners and occupants of problem residences and eventually ban occupants from residing and participating in drug activity in these places. At one location, the owner violated the terms of the Court Order, and the court forced the sale of the property. This case represented the first time the court ordered the sale of a property pursuant to a drug nuisance case filing. Strong City was instrumental in bringing together the community, BPD and city DHCD to implement this cutting-edge solution to street-level drug activity, an essential prerequisite to turning the neighborhood around.

Another turning point for Harwood came about in 2011, when then-Mayor Stephanie Rawlings-Blake announced the impending closure and subsequent privatization of two-dozen of the city's 55 recreation centers. The Barclay Recreation Center, attached to the Barclay School, was among those cited for closure due to its long history of poor maintenance. Recognizing the building's potential as a major asset, Strong City collaborated with residents to organize a community-wide meeting to discuss transforming Barclay Rec into a high-quality facility that could offer programs and services to enhance the quality of life in Harwood and its surrounding neighborhoods.

At the community's request, Strong City assumed management and led the efforts to rehabilitate the building. Johns Hopkins University granted Strong City three years of funding, and its Carey School of Business was recruited to lead the development of a business plan. Meanwhile, Strong City staff negotiated with City Schools and the Department of Recreation and Parks to formalize a Memorandum of Understanding that outlined its new role as a private manager.

With the three-year Johns Hopkins grant and an additional multi-year commitment from a private foundation, Strong City was able to hire Hannah Gardi as the full-time Community Center Director as well as hire a part-time Program Coordinator. Over the next year and a half, community volunteers and Strong City staff spent over 1,200 hours cleaning, painting, and marketing the building, which the community voted to rename the 29th Street Community Center.

Reopening and operating a recreation center was not something Strong City had ever planned on doing, but it fit seamlessly into the organization's holistic community development philosophy and provided ample opportunity to offer programs and services for all ages in a community that had lacked resources for so long.

Yet another big change for Harwood arrived in 2012, when Johns Hopkins announced its Homewood Community Partners Initiative (HCPI) – a $60 million plan seeded by $10 million from the university over several years in 10 neighborhoods immediately surrounding its Homewood campus, including Harwood.

In May 2013, more than 200 families and children attended the 29th Street Community Center's grand opening. The first summer programs were launched the following month, enrolling more than 200 youth. The Community Center gained considerable notice from community organizers in other parts of the city and country because of its intentionally inclusive model and efforts to attract and retain families in Harwood and the surrounding neighborhoods.

As of fall 2019, the Community Center was going strong, serving hundreds of youth and adults with mostly community-led programming at little or no cost, and had added an employment development component with several Youth After-School Coordinators.

"It was all tied together," said Strong City CEO Karen D. Stokes. "For example, our hope is that new parents who enjoy the Center will want to stay in the neighborhood and use the local public schools." She added, "The 29ᵗʰ Street Community Center is a new local anchor institution in Harwood."

> Reopening and operating a recreation center was not something Strong City had ever planned on doing, but it fit seamlessly into the organization's holistic community development philosophy.

Where We Are and Where We're Going

Strong City's work, via HCPI, with the Barclay School led to enormous dividends with the partnership between the school and the Johns Hopkins University Whiting School of Engineering – a clear example of Strong City's role as a "convener," connecting anchor institutions to community needs. Launched in 2015, this partnership led to the creation of the Barclay School's Engineering Lab, a multimillion-dollar, 10-year investment from Johns Hopkins, and a 10-year partnership between the Whiting School and Barclay. With this lab and its resources, every student entering Barclay as a pre-schooler will have 10 years of engineering education by the time they finish eighth grade.

This was possible due to Strong City's relationship with both the Barclay School and Johns Hopkins, leveraging our success in improving the school through Community School coordinators and bringing together partners at the Barclay School to secure this investment. (After a long and successful run, the Community Schools partnership between Strong City and the Barclay School ended in 2017; as of this writing, Strong City still sponsored Community School coordinators at the Margaret Brent, Govans, and Guilford schools.)

The Barclay School's exterior also got a boost to reflect the vibrant activity inside with the beautiful mosaic mural that adorns the school's entrance (a portion of which is featured on the cover of this book). Tamara Payne created the mural for her graduate program at the Maryland Institute College of Art (MICA). Strong City helped Tamara write a grant for the project, which was a collaboration with Barclay School pupils, local historian Jo Ann Robinson, and students from Johns Hopkins.

In fact, so many colorful tiled artworks created or inspired by Tamara (including the "Welcome to Harwood" sign at 25th and Barclay streets) began showing up around Harwood in the mid-2010s that some people began calling it the "neighborhood of mosaics." Another example is Tamara's "Butterfly Project" – the butterfly being a symbol of beauty and transformation that applies well to Harwood.

Tamara Payne's multifaceted relationship with Strong City over the years – as a community association president, fiscally sponsored community artist, block project organizer, and instructor at the 29th Street Community Center – is emblematic of Strong City's holistic, grassroots approach to organizing and empowering residents.

But all the positive developments in Harwood would not be enough to transform a neighborhood blighted by hundreds of vacant houses – and so, Strong City hastened its efforts around redevelopment.

While the Healthy Neighborhoods program had been successfully implemented on certain target blocks in Harwood, other blocks had vacancy rates well in excess of those permissible for Healthy Neighborhoods funding. "Nothing signals decline more clearly than the persistent problem of vacant houses," notes Peter Duvall, who had been spearheading strategic code enforcement efforts in Harwood since 2002.

By 2012, Strong City's work had helped reduce vacancies in Harwood from nearly 200 to 63, with a dozen under rehabilitation. This kind of outstanding progress attracted the City's attention. In May 2012, then-Baltimore City Housing Commissioner Paul Graziano publicly kicked off the demolition of nine properties on a predominantly vacant block in Harwood.

As one of the Mayor's Vacants to Value Community Development Cluster (CDC) areas, this block was a strategic zone undergoing major revitalization in an effort to increase investment and reduce the number of vacants in the area. "Harwood, like many of our blighted neighborhoods, has suffered from 50 years of disinvestment," Graziano said. "This didn't happen overnight, but our demolition today should signal anyone who is interested that the City is committed to making a major impact in this wonderful community."

The demolition was intended to create an opportunity for successful revitalization by making way for future development – which it did. In July 2013, Strong City was awarded a $500,000 grant from the National Conservation Initiative (NCI), which it used to provide gap funding to incentivize private developers in the renovation of 11 properties on Whitridge and Lorraine avenues. The developers, who had previously renovated several other properties on these blocks, committed to rebuilding immediately upon receipt of funds, which would lead to significant blight elimination within a relatively short period. Most of the $500,000 was used on the initial phase of the project to fix the exteriors and roofs of all 10 properties, quickly improving the attractiveness of the block.

"It is crucial to our neighborhood's future to have a strong base of homeownership in all parts of our community," wrote former Harwood Community Association President Myron Seay, in a letter of support for the redevelopment project, dubbed Whitridge Row. Maryland Attorney General Brian Frosh attended the project's 2015 unveiling. By the end of 2019, all the houses on Whitridge had sold.

That's gratifying to residents like Tamara Payne, who feels the love and care she has put into the neighborhood are producing results. "When I moved here, half my block was vacant and all of Whitridge was vacant," she recalls. "Now, the last three community association presidents have lived on Whitridge, and there are no vacants on my block."

Finally, what residents considered the "weakest" parts of Harwood started seeing a revival. Because most of the neighborhood was thriving again, the community, Strong City, and at least three developers were able to turn their attention to the small part of the neighborhood east of Greenmount Avenue, sometimes called "East Harwood." This area, still highly blighted, had a vacancy rate of over 50 percent at the end of 2019. But the project partners had acquired and begun renovation on over a dozen houses.

Additionally, Strong City helped write a Land Use Plan for the area that was turned into a rezoning ordinance introduced by City Councilwoman Mary Pat Clarke and approved in 2019. The ordinance rezones parcels along Greenmount Avenue to allow for the construction of an apartment building for seniors – a community objective. At this writing, the city was working to acquire properties at 27th and Greenmount for that purpose. In addition, six rowhomes in the neighborhood had been rehabbed and four more were under construction.

New residents moving in and legacy residents reinvesting in their homes have led Harwood to thrive again. Although 2019 was a tough year, with new vacants coming on line as fast as existing ones could be fixed, in general the success of code enforcement efforts in the neighborhood has been remarkable, with the number of vacant houses dropping over 85 percent since 2003, for a total of just 28 at the end of 2019.

People have noticed the change. In 2014, Harwood was rated by the national real estate company Redfin as Baltimore's second-hottest neighborhood – a far cry from the early 2000s. And Harwood's success has had citywide repercussions: The code enforcement efforts first rolled out there were integrated into the Vacants to Value code enforcement strategy now implemented in many parts of the city.

> New residents moving in and legacy residents reinvesting in their homes have led Harwood to thrive again.

Key Strategies: Harwood

1. **Strengthen the Neighborhood Public School.** In 2005, after many years of providing Ameri-Corps VISTAs as a resource to schools, Strong City received funding to implement a formal Community School model at the Barclay School, which increased its capacity to leverage and coordinate service delivery, manage volunteers, and engage parents and neighborhood residents in programs and activities that market the school as a desirable choice to families who might otherwise leave the neighborhood or city.

2. **Promote New Investment.** As local administrator for the Healthy Neighborhoods program, Strong City helped increase homeownership, investment, and curb appeal, and

improved physical condition and overall pride. Staff worked hard to market the neighborhood to connect people to loans that would help bring new residents and retain existing ones, while block improvement projects enhanced curb appeal.

3. **Strategic Code Enforcement.** Crucial to Harwood's revival, and closely connected to promoting new investment, has been Strong City's long-term, successful partnership with Baltimore City's Code Enforcement Legal Section. Strong City's Strategic Code Enforcement program targets key dilapidated properties for attention from the city and has become a citywide model.

4. **Increase Leadership Capacity.** Strong City's fiscal sponsorship provided training, resources, and assistance for the Harwood Community Association to build and improve the neighborhood and resolve problems by utilizing best practices and advocacy strategies, and accessing city services and resources.

5. **Bring a New Community Anchor Online.** In 2013, the abandoned Barclay Rec Center reopened as the 29th Street Community Center, a new anchor institution in Harwood operated by Strong City and serving hundreds of families weekly with low- or no-cost programming, most of it community-led.

Harwood Timeline/Fact Sheet

- Starting in the 1970s, AmeriCorps VISTAs sponsored by Strong City do family engagement and after-school programming at Harwood's Barclay Elementary/Middle School

- Strong City helps launch the Barclay Brent Education Corporation (BBEC), dedicated to improving the Barclay and Margaret Brent schools

- In 2005, Strong City implements the Community Schools model at Barclay, expanding on the work VISTAs had been doing there for decades

- Johns Hopkins University, Goucher College, Loyola University Maryland, and Maryland Institute College of Art supply volunteers to the new Community School

- Strong City secures grants for a variety of block projects through its work with Healthy Neighborhoods

- Strong City supports the Harwood Community Association (HCA) as it builds leadership capacity; Strong City becomes the HCA's fiscal sponsor

- In 2009, Strong City secures funding from the Goldseker Foundation to launch the Great Schools Charles Village initiative, a successor to the BBEC

- In 2012, the community names Strong City as new operator of the abandoned Barclay

Recreation Center in Harwood; it reopens in 2013 as the 29th Street Community Center and proceeds to serve 400 adults and children weekly with free or low-cost, community-led programming

- In 2012, Johns Hopkins University launches the Homewood Community Partners Initiative (HCPI) in 10 neighborhoods, including Harwood; Strong City plays key role as intermediary between Johns Hopkins and the neighborhoods
- Strong City supports the work of community artist and neighborhood leader Tamara Payne through support of her community art projects, her leadership of the HCA, and her classes at the Community Center
- Strong City secures a Healthy Neighborhoods grant for Ilchester Avenue residents to enter the Charles Village Painted Ladies contest; all 10 entries win first place
- In 2012, Strong City partners with the University of Maryland social work school to hire an outreach worker in Harwood
- Harwood Halloween, with Strong City's support, becomes a pivotal event bringing the neighborhood together
- Strong City continues to hold block captain trainings and Neighborhood Leaders forums in Harwood

- Strong City, via HCPI, nurtures a relationship between Johns Hopkins and Harwood's Barclay School that results in the university funding a multi-million-dollar engineering lab and curriculum at the school
- In 2013, Strong City wins a $500,000 grant from the National Conservation Initiative (NCI) for the Whitridge Row project, a renovation of 11 vacant properties on Whitridge and Lorraine avenues
- In 2014, Redfin calls Harwood Baltimore's second-hottest neighborhood
- By the end of 2019, Strong City's strategic code enforcement has helped reduce vacancies in Harwood to fewer than 30, an 85% drop since 2003

Whitridge Avenue was almost entirely vacant before Strong City's Peter Duvall won a $500,000 grant to incentivize developers to renovate 11 properties on Whitridge and Lorraine avenues. By the end of 2019, all houses on the newly dubbed "Whitridge Row" had been sold.

Tamara Payne's multifaceted relationship with Strong City – as community association president, fiscally sponsored community artist, block project organizer, and 29th Street Community Center instructor – speaks to the organization's holistic, grassroots approach.

Harwood residents asked Strong City to lead the renovation and management of an abandoned city rec center, which reopened in 2013 as the 29th Street Community Center. The Center serves hundreds weekly with mostly community-led programming at little or no cost.

In its role as intermediary, Strong City helps forge ties between anchor institutions and local communities. An example is Johns Hopkins' multi-million-dollar investment at the Barclay School in Harwood, allowing all students to receive 10 years of education in engineering.

REMINGTON

Background

Remington is a historically working-class neighborhood in north-central Baltimore well known for its mix of single-family rowhouses, small businesses, industry, major streets, and green space. Its boundaries include the Johns Hopkins University on the north, and Howard Street, a major north-south artery, on the east. Heavy east-west traffic travels via 28th and 29th streets through the heart of Remington to and from the Jones Falls Expressway (JFX), a major interstate that rests directly above the Jones Falls river.

In the 1880s, Baltimore's population grew, and Remington was seen as well situated for development – peppered with textile mills, iron foundries, and water-powered factories that provided "an enormous amount of stone for the building of Baltimore."[XI] As the population grew with the mills and quarries, America's first electric railway, built in 1885, brought new residents, and Remington was annexed into the city in 1888. In the years that followed, thousands of rowhouses were built, as were notable landmarks in or near Remington including Guardian Angel Episcopal Church (1898), Johns Hopkins University Homewood

Campus (1925), Stieff Silver factory (1925), and the Baltimore Museum of Art (1929).[XII]

Remington's reputation as an attractive suburban area known for location, jobs, and convenient transportation via railroad and streetcars continued well into the mid-20th century. The neighborhood experienced redlining in the 1930s, likely due to the presence of Italian immigrants and a significant minority of African-Americans. As many industries, including quarries and cotton duck mills, slowed down in the 1930s and 1940s, residents found work with canning and silverware factories, some large-scale development projects, and new auto dealerships. In the 1950s, Remington's streetcar lines began closing in preparation for construction of the JFX, which opened in 1962 near Remington's westernmost boundary.[XIII]

By the 1960s and 1970s, most mills and quarries had shut down, and factory jobs declined. Many longtime residents moved away, while those remaining often struggled. In 1965, the resident-led Remington Improvement Association (RIA) was formed to address these critical issues. Over the next decade, the RIA worked to expand services, organized regular cleanups and beautification projects, advocated for the construction of two playgrounds and a multi-purpose center, and published a newsletter. By 1976, the RIA was considered by most residents to be "the local mechanism for action."[XIV]

That same year, the RIA partnered with Strong City Baltimore to produce the *Remington Fact Book*, with the goals of defining Remington and establishing a basis for future decisions. Statistics gathered regarding population, economy, housing, and existing services were startling. One of the bleakest facts: Roughly 80 percent of Remington residents over age 24 had not completed high school.

Vacant housing, unemployment, drug abuse, rats, and lack of public transportation had all become areas of great concern. Basic amenities like a local school or public library were located many blocks away in the Charles Village neighborhood. While Remington contained two zoned business districts, there simply wasn't enough retail diversity to meet the needs of its residents. Many of these problems would follow Remington well into the late 1990s. As its population continued to decrease, illegal drug use and the crime that came with it grew.

By the early 2000s, Remington, like many Baltimore neighborhoods, began to see an influx of young residents seeking affordable housing. Many were Johns Hopkins employees and students who considered Remington convenient and inexpensive. Recognizing this trend, a group of key university faculty and staff came together to examine what role the university as an anchor institution could play in making Remington a safer, more attractive place for current and future residents.

Seeing it as crucial that their efforts stimulate investment while maintaining the neighborhood's mixed-income character, Johns Hopkins chose Strong City Baltimore as its lead partner, whose task would be to spearhead a community building effort that would ultimately bring about sustainable, results-driven revitalization. Or, in the words of Pastor Alice Bassett-Jellema (now deceased) at Guardian Angel Episcopal Church, "To help people remember how to be in a neighborhood."

> Vacant housing, unemployment, drug abuse, rats, and lack of public transportation had all become areas of great concern. Many of these problems would follow Remington well into the late 1990s.

Approaching the Work

"Remington would benefit from the work of an experienced, paid organizer," wrote consultant Paul Brophy in a 2004 report on the neighborhood. Brophy, who specialized in advancing social and economic gains through affordable housing, had been engaged by Johns Hopkins to frame an approach to a stronger partnership between the university and Remington. After conducting extensive interviews with key stakeholders in the community and collecting data on the housing market in Remington, Brophy presented a baseline of information that was intended to stimulate an action plan.

At the time, housing prices in Baltimore were on the upswing, indicating a resurgence in homebuyers' perception that Baltimore was a good place to live. In nearby Charles Village, where many Johns Hopkins students and employees traditionally lived, sales prices for homes had increased by 140 percent in just three years. Rents were rising, too. And while Remington real estate experienced a bit of an upswing, its median price of homes sold in 2004 was still only $68,000.[XV]

Remington was seen as risky to new investors and businesses due to its generally fragile economics and fragmented sense of community. There was no business association, nor – following the demise of the RIA – was there any "highly regarded neighborhood organization that [spoke] for the neighborhood."[XVI]

The Remington Neighborhood Alliance (RNA), formed in 2000 by a small cohort of residents, was generally regarded as hostile toward any new neighborhood developments. Remington was at a crossroads and could easily have stagnated or regressed further without some kind of intervention.

In 2005, in a move that would prove pivotal, Strong City Baltimore hired a full-time community organizer to facilitate the Remington Community Engagement Initiative. The goal of the Initiative was to implement high-impact projects that strategically addressed the needs and potential of Remington. Strong City identified five project areas within which they would continually work with community and city partners, residents, and businesses to achieve this goal: community leadership and neighborhood building; housing and real estate; streetscapes, cleaning, and greening; supporting good businesses; and providing quality educational opportunities.

All of these project areas served as key ingredients in the rebuilding of Remington. Through its community organizing efforts, Strong City mobilized residents into a coordinated group of active citizens who collectively worked on behalf of their shared self-interest. As a result, a committed network of people emerged fully prepared to take on projects that would bring real, measurable progress to their neighborhood.

From Vision to Action

In 2005, Strong City launched its first community organizing efforts in Remington with an extensive door-knocking campaign, followed by community-wide meetings held at the Guardian Angel Episcopal Church. Seen as a reliable and trusted community anchor, the church offered Strong City an access point into the neighborhood by helping publicize meetings and soliciting input from residents, many of whom were among Remington's most vulnerable. Some residents were eager to make big changes, while others felt defeated by the neighborhood's continued decline even as they also feared potential gentrification (a fear that would be borne out in the eyes of some, including Pastor Bassett-Jellema).

Over the next four years, organizers worked closely with residents to identify both short- and long-term goals that could eventually be integrated into an achievable neighborhood plan. One of the most important changes during this period was the emergence of a new, progressive-minded community organization, the Greater Remington Improvement Association (GRIA).

Eric Imhof, a founder of GRIA, recalled that Strong City "was instrumental in moving us from the phase of getting together and doing cleanups to really organizing." Key to the success of this work was providing technical assistance and support for developing a positive relationship between residents and city government, businesses, nonprofit organizations, and outside stakeholders.

Strong City served as a convener and bridge-builder, connecting GRIA with institutions and resources including the Community Law Center (CLC), Johns Hopkins, and various agencies of city government, such as the police and housing department. Having the support of Strong City, an established, respected organization, "helped give us some confidence – helped encourage us so that we would have the ability to get stuff done," Imhof said. "That was crucial for us."

As this work unfolded, so did a series of community-building initiatives intended to keep residents engaged as well as to meet their expressed needs. Among these was an annual back-to-school celebration and supply drive; a holiday toy giveaway sponsored by Deutsche Bank USA; the Liberty Property Trust Volunteer Day, which provided home repairs; and the Johns Hopkins APO fraternity Winterization Project, which built relationships between residents and Johns Hopkins students.

> Strong City mobilized residents into a coordinated group of active citizens who collectively worked on behalf of their shared self-interest. One of the most important changes was the emergence of a new, progressive-minded community organization, the Greater Remington Improvement Association (GRIA).

One notable accomplishment from that inaugural year was the reinstitution of a neighborhood newsletter. Sponsored in part by Johns Hopkins and the Episcopal Housing Corporation, *The Remington Community Newsletter* was intended to inform residents about resources, events, and programs. Residents and other local stakeholders were invited to contribute to the newsletter, which was printed and distributed monthly to an average of 1,200 homes. (Technical challenges forced a suspension of the *Newsletter* in spring 2018; GRIA formed a Communications Committee in 2019 with the hope of getting a bimonthly publication back online soon.)

Also in 2005, Strong City served as a fiscal sponsor and coordinator for Open Society Institute Fellow Peter Babcox, whose Remington Public Gardens (RPG) project trained local youth in creating and caring for "pocket gardens" throughout the neighborhood. Participating youth received stipends for their work, which was often accomplished alongside community volunteers.

In 2006, Strong City established a partnership with the Maryland Institute College of Art's (MICA) Community Arts Partnership Program, which hosted a five-week summer arts camp that culminated with a youth-led community exhibition and the construction of several community murals. That same year, Strong City organizer Victoria Der created a five-week dance class in collaboration with a local teacher. And Strong City's partnership with the Baltimore Tennis Patrons provided free tennis lessons to kids twice a week for eight weeks each summer. Funding for organizing in Remington came from Johns Hopkins, Goldseker, and an individual donor who committed to supporting this work for five years.

An important turning point for Remington took place in 2007, when it was added to the Healthy Neighborhoods program. As the administrator of Healthy Neighborhoods for north-central Baltimore, Strong City applied for this designation to make Remington eligible for rehabilitation loans and block project grant funds, while also marketing the neighborhood to potential homebuyers. Median sales prices in Remington had risen to $175,950 – a vast improvement over where the market had been just three years earlier.

Meanwhile, at the block level, resident-led improvements were under way, including the installation of porch lights, potted plants, and other small-scale physical improvements that united neighbors in a common cause. Resident block captains trained by Strong City staff managed each project in collaboration with other residents.

Remington was finally at the brink of real, tangible change and had reached a critical mass of resident interest and ability, marked by GRIA's emergence as a widely supported and fully established resident-led community group, with Strong City serving as its fiscal sponsor. GRIA had identified the areas of housing, planning, and greening as priorities and was already making considerable steps toward addressing each area.

With a robust neighborhood organization finally in place, Strong City's organizing role changed to providing technical assistance in the areas of grant writing and research, planning of improvement projects, and expertise in housing and code enforcement. With help from additional Strong City staff and partners in the Baltimore City Council President's Office and the Housing Department, a list of vacant and non-code-compliant properties was developed, and several meetings with high-level city officials and entities took place.

Remington recognized the challenges it faced in making immediate, visible impact. For example, nine of the properties identified as non-code-compliant needed to be transferred from the Housing Authority of Baltimore City (which purchased them with federal funds) to the Mayor and City Council – a process that could take up to two years.

In the meantime, Strong City was raising additional funds to implement improvement projects on some of Remington's most-challenging blocks that were not yet eligible for Healthy Neighborhoods funds. Widespread, small-scale greening initiatives were also in full force, including a community garden that was developed across eight vacant lots, a resident-operated greenhouse, and a white-roof initiative that would offer residents a low-cost solution to cutting energy bills.

In 2008, Strong City and GRIA approached the Neighborhood Design Center (NDC), which provides access to pro bono design services in underserved communities, regarding the feasibility of developing a Remington master plan. The NDC encouraged GRIA to apply, with support from Strong City. GRIA's main goal in developing a master plan was to provide an avenue for residents to share their ideas for Remington's future, which would then be woven into a vision for the community.

GRIA had organized itself into committees focused on particular areas or projects. Once their application to the NDC was approved, a steering committee was established to host a series of team meetings and community workshops that focused on the planning process.

The steering committee worked with Remington residents, community leaders, and the NDC to document what residents liked about Remington and what they thought could be improved. Steering committee members held one-on-one conversations with residents; hosted a resident art exhibition, *Remington Stories: Images from the Past, Visions for the Future;* and kept people up to date through flyers, email, newsletters, and website postings.

By 2009, the steering committee and the NDC had held five monthly planning sessions attended by residents, businesses, local nonprofits, faith-based organizations, and elected officials.[XVII]

GRIA was finally ready to begin drafting a Remington master plan, organized by five main themes reflecting the ideas collected: identity, housing, open and green space, mobility, and neighborhood business.

Another major turning point for Remington was the acquisition of the longtime vacant Census Building (formerly the H.F. Miller and Son Tin Box and Can Manufacturing Plant) by Seawall Development Co., a privately held real estate operating company. To purchase the property at Remington's border with Charles Village, Seawall needed historic tax credits that could only be secured with a nonprofit entity.

Seawall approached Strong City with a plan to redevelop the building as Miller's Court, which would provide affordable living for public school teachers and office space for area nonprofits. With GRIA's approval, Strong City provided collaborative support and consistent community engagement on this $20 million project, which welcomed its first residents in 2009.

Having a quality neighborhood school was a critical factor in ensuring that Remington could become a desirable place for families to live. Strong City assigned several VISTAs over the years to coordinate services and volunteers to strengthen Remington's closest public school, Margaret Brent Elementary/Middle School in Charles Village, before winning funding in 2011 to transform it into a "Community School."

Schools with that designation offer wraparound services to students and families with an integrated focus on academics, health and social services, youth and community development, and community engagement. With this funding, Strong City was able to place a full-time Community School Site Coordinator at Margaret Brent to assist with bringing much-needed resources to students and their families.

By 2010, Remington's population had risen for the first time in 80 years.[XVIII] Streetscaping, beautification, greening, and community cleanup efforts had brought visible changes to the landscape. Healthy Neighborhoods had spurred over $400,000 worth of investment, and residents had completed more than 30 block projects. GRIA had created a mission statement, launched a website, taken over management of *The Remington Community Newsletter*, and actively participated in multiple planning and housing endeavors. Remington was finally regaining its status as a vibrant urban community.

> By 2010, Remington's population had risen for the first time in 80 years. Remington was finally regaining its status as a vibrant urban community.

Where We Are and Where We're Going

Community organizing laid the groundwork for positive change in Remington, whose momentum would only continue to grow. As it did, and in keeping with our guiding philosophy, Strong City scaled back its role in the mid-2010s, while GRIA and its committees took the driver's seat.

Capitalizing on this momentum, Seawall privately purchased at least 17 rowhouses in Remington and also won a bidding process to rehab nine city-owned houses in 2012.[XIX]

They then built Miller's Square – a series of completely renovated historic homes that were sold at affordable rates ($100,000 to $200,000). These homes were marketed to young professionals and families, and in particular to teachers who had previously been renting space at Miller's Court. Upgrading to an affordable and beautiful home was pitched as a great investment not just in property but also in the community.

In 2013, GRIA published its first draft of the Remington Neighborhood Plan – the result of a five-year collaboration with residents and stakeholders who attended dozens of community meetings, planning sessions, and workshops. Among their key priorities for the neighborhood was bringing back corner stores, requiring a comprehensive rezoning of targeted properties that allowed for small-scale commercial use. This rezoning would make way for new businesses that embodied what Remington envisioned for itself: bike shops, cafes, florists, bookstores, and art galleries.[XX]

GRIA submitted a request to rezone 12 corner store properties in the citywide rezoning process known as Transform Baltimore, hoping that it would be quickly passed and new local businesses could fill vacant corners and create jobs. The city's rezoning process, which was under debate at the time, stalled GRIA's plans, but in spring 2015 GRIA organized a cohort of volunteer residents around advocating for their proposed rezoning. They petitioned and collected more than 200 signatures, held meetings, flyered, distributed documents that explained the zoning change, and testified before the planning commission and Baltimore City Council, which recognized these efforts as unprecedented in size and scope.

By December 2015, the rezoning ordinance was passed, but the RNA, a competing community organization, successfully challenged it, delaying the ordinance's implementation. GRIA then redoubled its efforts with a new, meticulously crafted City Council ordinance, and simultaneously lobbied to ensure that the corner properties would be zoned for commercial use under Transform Baltimore. They won on both counts, resulting in five businesses opening, one under construction, and more in the planning stages, as of late 2019.

As for the Remington Neighborhood Plan, 10 years after those initial meetings, it was officially accepted by the city Planning Commission in early 2018. "It's good for us – it means we can start getting some better stuff for our community," said Ryan Flanigan, former GRIA president. He noted that having the Plan in place makes it easier for GRIA to work with the city, get the attention of officials, and unlock capital funding for issues that matter to residents, such as traffic calming and investments in housing and parks.

Another milestone came in October 2017, when GRIA was able to hire a full-time Community Organizer, with support from Johns Hopkins, Seawall, and Price Modern, to uphold Remington's diversity, vibrancy, and community connectedness by helping to implement GRIA's Strategic Plan and the Remington Neighborhood Plan. Going forward, GRIA has decided the community would be best served by switching to a full-time Executive Director to develop and execute programs and services that work toward GRIA's goals and mission as envisioned by the two plans.

The turnaround in Remington has raised issues that seemed inconceivable 20 years ago. The neighborhood boasts rehabbed rowhomes, new apartments, restaurants, and projects such as the mixed-use development Remington Row and the R. House food hall. An innovative concept, the Remington Storefront Challenge, was created to activate vacant and underutilized retail spaces and support local entrepreneurs by offering rent-free retail spaces for 12 to 24 months to new businesses in need of a jump start.

Concerned about the impact of development on low-income residents, GRIA is determined to preserve affordable housing, with Flanigan and others working with local nonprofits to develop a Community Land Trust in Remington as part of a pilot project involving six city neighborhoods.

But Pastor Alice Bassett-Jellema said that such efforts come too late for residents forced to leave the neighborhood due to rising rents, noting that "Definitions of what is 'better' vary on the basis of who you are." While the Homestead Tax Credit largely protects homeowners from large tax increases when property values rise, there is still a lack of meaningful protections for renters. (Tragically, Pastor Bassett-Jellema died of a brain tumor in November 2019 at age 62, after serving Guardian Angel church for 22 years.)

Strong City's grassroots community organizing efforts helped Remington get to where it is today. The success of the neighborhood – frequently named as one of Baltimore's most desirable – results from an organizing model that addressed its risk factors and intentionally built upon its assets.

> The success of the neighborhood – frequently named as one of Baltimore's most desirable – results from an organizing model that addressed its risk factors and intentionally built upon its assets.

Key Strategies: Remington

1. **Community Leadership and Neighborhood Building.** Strong City worked with community residents to facilitate local leadership devel-

opment and the formation of a new, inclusive community group, the Greater Remington Improvement Association (GRIA). Strong City also spearheaded a series of neighborhood strengthening projects led by residents or done in partnership with community stakeholders.

2. **Housing and Real Estate.** To ensure quality and affordable rental properties, homeownership opportunities for low- and middle-income residents, and the identification and improvement of problem properties, Strong City developed a plan to create new, mixed-income housing opportunities (both renovations and new construction). A partnership was established with Healthy Neighborhoods, making Remington eligible for acquisition and rehabilitation loans as well as block improvement grants. Meanwhile, the Community Land Trust spearheaded by Ryan Flanigan offers an innovative and promising housing alternative.

3. **Streetscapes, Cleaning, and Greening.** Strong City worked closely with residents and community stakeholders to reduce blight, complete street and sidewalk repairs, and improve lighting and cleanliness. Resident committees focusing on issues such as rats, sewage, trash pickup, and park renewal worked with local and citywide partners to keep Remington clean and green.

4. **Supporting Good Businesses.** Significant commercial vacancies prompted partnerships with local businesses, the Mayor's Office of Neighborhoods, and the Department of Planning to conduct outreach and fill vacant spaces with new businesses. A GRIA sub-committee served as a functional business association that recruited new businesses and developed large projects.

5. **Quality Educational Opportunities.** Strong City assigned AmeriCorps VISTAs to Margaret Brent Elementary/Middle School, before winning funding in 2011 to turn it into a Community School, bringing much-needed resources to students and their families. Margaret Brent also benefited greatly from capital improvements and beautification funded by the Homewood Community Partners Initiative (HCPI).

Remington Timeline/Fact Sheet

- In the early 2000s, Johns Hopkins University chooses Strong City as its lead partner in community building efforts in Remington
- In 2005, Strong City hires a full-time community organizer to facilitate Johns Hopkins' Remington Community Engagement Initiative focused on building neighborhood leadership, housing and real estate, streetscape

improvements, business development, and education

- Strong City works with residents to launch a new, inclusive neighborhood group, which ultimately becomes the Greater Remington Improvement Association (GRIA)
- Strong City helps launch the monthly *Remington Community Newsletter*
- In 2005, Strong City fiscally sponsors Open Society Institute-Baltimore (OSI) Fellow Peter Babcox's Remington Gardens Project
- In 2006, Strong City takes on a number of projects in Remington, including a partnership with the Maryland Institute College of Art (MICA) on a five-week arts summer camp and the creation of several murals; a dance class offered by a Strong City organizer and a local teacher; and a partnership with Baltimore Tennis Patrons to provide free tennis lessons for local kids
- In 2007, Strong City successfully advocates for Remington's inclusion in the Healthy Neighborhoods program
- In 2007, block captains trained by Strong City oversee a series of street improvements
- As GRIA's fiscal sponsor, Strong City supports the neighborhood organization with grant writing, research, code enforcement, and more
- In 2008, Strong City and GRIA approach the

Neighborhood Design Center about creating a Remington master plan to establish a vision to guide Remington's future

- In 2009, Miller's Court opens as teacher housing and nonprofit offices, redeveloped by Seawall Development; Strong City secures the project's historic tax credits and provides community engagement
- Seawall goes on to create workforce housing at Miller's Square and Remington Row, and develops the popular food hall R. House
- In 2010, Remington's population increases for first time in 80 years
- In 2018, a decade after discussions began, the City Council finally adopts the Remington Neighborhood Plan, allowing the neighborhood greater access to city services and capital funding
- *Baltimore City Paper* names Remington Baltimore's "top up and coming neighborhood"

Seawall Development transformed an old auto shop into the R. House food hall, which draws people from all over the city to Remington. Seawall also redeveloped a vacant building on Howard Street into housing for teachers, with Strong City helping secure needed tax credits.

In the mid-2000s, Strong City served as a fiscal sponsor and coordinator for Open Society Institute-Baltimore Fellow Peter Babcox, whose Remington Public Gardens project trained local youth in creating and caring for "pocket gardens" throughout the neighborhood.

Although not located in Remington, Margaret Brent Elementary/Middle is the neighborhood's closest school. Strong City won funding to place a full-time Community School Coordinator at Margaret Brent to assist with bringing resources to students and families.

Seawall Development built Miller's Square, a cluster of completely renovated historic homes that were sold at affordable rates ($100,000 to $200,000) with marketing support from Strong City. These homes were marketed to young professionals and families.

YORK ROAD PARTNERSHIP

Background

Situated between 39th Street and the northern city line and Charles Street and The Alameda, the York Road Corridor has long been known for its array of retail businesses. It is also a kind of residential "spine" that connects more than 20 neighborhoods. For many decades, York Road has been a dividing line for race and class. To its west are largely white communities that are some of the wealthiest in Baltimore City, including the formerly racially covenanted neighborhoods of Guilford and Homeland. To its east is a mix of African-American working-class neighborhoods with pockets of poverty.

In the 1940s and 50s, the York Road Corridor became the epicenter of what was called the Greater Govans community by anchoring itself as a shopping destination that catered to surrounding suburban developments: Movie theaters, taverns, drugstores, banks, restaurants, service stations, and specialty shoe and clothing stores were among the many businesses built at that time. But as with many once-thriving sections of Baltimore, by the 1980s and '90s, York Road suffered a steep downturn marked by empty storefronts and drug trafficking in the commercial corridor, and a rise in crime and vacancy, along with declining home values, in the east-side black neighborhoods.

Strong City had a longstanding role in supporting a handful of community-led entities working to improve the corridor. These groups, contending with everything from crime to trash removal, did not always agree on priorities. Former Strong City Executive Director Bill Miller recalls several failed partnership programs and community meetings that were so divisive, city entities refused to attend. After continued disagreements over planning potential, Strong City was asked by a group of neighborhoods and businesses to intervene and moderate a community planning session.

In 1995, volunteer representatives from both sides of the Corridor's neighborhoods came together to form the York Road Partnership (YRP) – an umbrella organization that unites 20 Baltimore neighborhoods and institutions across a historical race and income divide to work together on common quality-of-life issues. They identified traffic, crime, trash, liquor license violations, and open-air drug markets as top priorities and quickly set to work on what would become one of the most diverse partnerships among neighborhood associations, nonprofit organizations, businesses, and religious and educational institutions in Baltimore City's history.

Approaching the Work

At its inception, YRP founders created three Action Groups – Residential, York Road, and Economic Development – as well as a list of short and long-term goals with time frames. They also formed a handful of committees, each of which has its own focus, though their work is intricately linked. Over the years, the YRP leadership encouraged people with energy to join committees or start new ones in line with agreed-upon priorities.

In 2002, the Baltimore City Planning Department launched the Strategic Neighborhood Action Plan (SNAP) program to create comprehensive plans for select "clusters" of neighborhoods throughout the city. YRP applied and was competitively accepted in February 2003. Subsequent community-wide meetings identified areas of community interests, concerns, and opportunities.

The planning process that followed included public forums and dozens of meetings, which helped YRP establish a vision vetted by the community for how the area should change and grow. In collaboration with the Govanstowne Business Association, YRP drafted a SNAP plan, which identified both assets and challenges in the areas of housing and neighborhood revitalization, commercial revitalization and economic development, open space and recreation, public safety, transportation, and community building. This plan was presented to the membership in December 2003.

Over the next several months, this draft was revised, edited, and regrouped into different categories, and goals were prioritized. Conflict arose over recommendations for the commercial corridor, eventually resulting in the business association withdrawing from the partnership over disagreements about code enforcement priorities and the fear of revitalization costing too much for small businesses.

A SNAP steering committee met with city representatives and proposed forging partnerships with several city agencies. A revised draft of the SNAP Plan was adopted by YRP and presented to the Mayor's Cabinet in July 2004. The city officially adopted YRP's plan in February 2006.

From Vision to Action

In 2005, Radnor-Winston neighborhood resident Karen DeCamp was elected President of the York Road Partnership. Karen, who was encouraged by the YRP's former President Jason Canapp to stand for election, had years of experience with grassroots organizing and advocacy and had served as President of the Radnor-Winston Neighborhood Association. Her vision was to grow YRP into a sophisticated and well-organized entity with the collective power and the capacity to leverage the resources of local anchor institutions, including Loyola University Maryland, Notre Dame of Maryland University, and local churches.

"I decided it was best to just name the divide," Karen said in reference to the corridor's race and class disparities. "I wanted this to be an organization that was honest about what separated us, but ultimately brought people together across that race and class divide to work on the issues we all cared about."

> "I wanted this to be an organization that was honest about what separated us, but ultimately brought people together across that race and class divide to work on the issues we all cared about."
>
> – *Karen DeCamp, former President of the York Road Partnership*

By 2007, YRP had representation from 25 neighborhoods and organizations, and their monthly meetings had become one of the most diverse forums in the city. YRP began advocating for revitalization efforts in key areas throughout the corridor, particularly those with problem properties. Among such properties was 5315 York Road, the site of at least two now-closed grocery stores. The Baltimore Development Corporation (BDC) rebuffed YRP's requests to use eminent domain to redevelop this problematic parcel. In 2005, a Family Dollar store had signed a long-term lease to use two of three of the vacant spaces in a nearby building and promised a small dairy and refrigerated food section.

At the time, the neighborhood was in great need of a convenient fresh food store. But within just a few months it became clear that the property owners cared little about maintenance and upkeep, as trash overflow and litter became an ongoing issue, especially for residents who lived nearby. YRP, through letters and meetings, urged the owners to maintain the property. When that didn't work, YRP requested that the city take legal action, which it did by fining Family Dollar $2,000 for a code violation and securing a legal agreement to keep the property clean. Ongoing work to watchdog that property has continued, with periodic city fines and health department closures. Woodbourne-McCabe neighborhood resident and YRP Leadership Committee member Phyllis Gilmore was especially vigilant in demanding accountability from Family Dollar.

With Karen DeCamp at the helm, YRP also ramped up its efforts to monitor liquor establishments and liquor board hearings. A 2007 article in *The Baltimore Messenger* about one problem store quoted residents' complaints that "customers hang out front all day, get drunk, throw bottles in the street and cause problems in the neighborhoods."[XXI]

YRP focused on stores and markets that had garnered reputations as problem businesses. With representation from the Community Law Center (CLC), the partnership took aggressive action against bars and liquor stores through petitioning, forcing liquor license transfers, and in some cases ensuring that businesses were closed for good. YRP successfully opposed liquor license transfers and moving licenses to other areas of the city.

YRP has a strong history of helping communities along the corridor deal with problem establishments that are magnets for crime, loitering and trash. Starting in 2007 with a request from the Richnor Springs neighborhood, YRP worked to decrease the number of liquor licenses on the corridor, learning how to organize people to challenge the City Liquor Board. This work was highly energizing and popular among YRP members. With the help of the CLC and knowledgeable YRP members, YRP developed a standard Memorandum of Understanding (MOU) for proprietors of new liquor establishments to sign to gain the support of YRP and the communities where such establishments are located. MOUs protect neighborhoods by restricting bad business practices such as early morning hours and trash issues, and require engagement with the community, better lighting, security, and protections against underage drinking.

Also in 2007, Karen DeCamp joined Strong City as a staff person working on community and school strengthening. In this position, Karen was able to leverage Strong City's connections and partnerships to benefit YRP. Strong City had held a position on YRP's leadership committee since the partnership's inception, and as such provided technical assistance, advice, and training for its members on organizing, advocacy, and code enforcement.

Vacant properties in the YRP neighborhoods were of great concern, with concentrations of severely blighted homes in Pen Lucy and Woodbourne-McCabe. With Habitat for Humanity already working on a set of vacant homes, YRP's chair of its Housing and Neighborhood Revitalization Committee, Dan Ellis (then representing Pen Lucy Action Network as its Executive Director), knew that YRP needed an understanding of the vacant home situation corridor-wide.

Dan manually mapped every vacant home using a list provided by the Housing Department. What he found was a stunning concentration of vacant properties: 40 within three blocks of McCabe Avenue – many owned by the city – including a good number with dangerous conditions such as collapsing porches and sanitation violations.

The YRP leadership agreed on a strategy to work with the Woodbourne-McCabe neighborhood, leveraging the collective power of all the YRP member neighborhoods and groups to make three asks of the Housing Department:

1. Clean up and enforce code on vacant properties;
2. Consolidate ownership, having the city acquire the vacants it didn't already own;
3. Bundle as many vacant properties as possible and offer them for development for home-ownership (not rentals, which it was felt would destabilize the neighborhood).

YRP worked with then-City Councilman Kenneth Harris (now deceased) to bring then-Baltimore City Housing Commissioner Paul Graziano and his staff on a walk-through of the neighborhood. YRP made the case that this level of blight was unacceptable. The Commissioner and his staff were shocked at the conditions on the McCabe blocks and noted their proximity to upper-income Homeland.

After making these demands, working with Councilman Harris, and demonstrating the power of YRP in several highly attended partnership meetings, YRP succeeded in getting the city to agree to its demands, and the work began. At this point, YRP had clearly earned the respect of the Housing Commissioner and his deputies.

The process that followed took several years of twists and turns. In particular, consolidation of ownership and code enforcement were long processes, and the plan to offer homes to a developer was delayed by the fall of the housing market. As of early 2020, Habitat for Humanity of the Chesapeake was transforming three blocks of McCabe Avenue into homes for low-income owners.

While YRP continued to advocate for the vision in its SNAP plan, leaders began to realize that the 2004 plan had been largely shelved by the city and was not driving agency priorities along the corridor as planned. In an August 2007 letter to then-Mayor Sheila Dixon, Karen DeCamp noted YRP's accomplishments to date and pleaded for stronger revitalization. "Now we need the city to step up anew and prioritize these issues, using the SNAP plan to guide its efforts," she wrote.

Streetscape improvements were also identified as a high priority, with a committee formed to watchdog the city/state streetscaping work (which after delays took over a decade to implement). Spearheaded by local resident and retired Loyola University professor Helene Perry, the committee strove to enhance the York Road corridor by ensuring the streetscape was attractive and green, and walkable and safe for pedestrians and cyclists.

The committee advocated for and maintained public spaces on the corridor and in neighborhoods, and worked to ensure that bus services and facilities were available, accessible and convenient (including advocating for bus shelters). It brought together people with interest in enhancing the appearance of the corridor through greening, and who had expertise in landscaping, urban ecology and environmental design.

Many new trees along the corridor were a result of door-to-door work of the committee members asking property owners to consent to a tree being planted. The committee also engaged thousands of hours of volunteer time to clean up the corridor, mulch trees, and plant annuals and perennials.

A special project involving many Loyola University and Friends School volunteers has been the Govans Urban Forest. Trash and invasive weeds were removed, trees were labeled, and curbside plantings and signage were added – all with the goal of retaining a native forest area in the community.

Also, through the city's Anchor Institutions strategy in the mid-2010s, Loyola received city and state funding to complete a series of "Bmore Birds" murals along York Road, as well as the "Welcome to Govans" signage at the southern and northern ends of the commercial corridor. This was done in partnership with the YRP and the Govanstowne Business Association.

Strong City had built a powerful relationship with Loyola University Maryland, one of Strong City's founding partners and among the most influential anchor institutions within YRP's footprint. Karen

DeCamp urged Loyola Vice President for Advancement Terry Sawyer to consider hiring a staff person to focus on working with YRP to improve York Road.

In early 2008, representatives from Loyola began meeting with YRP to discuss how they could establish a formal partnership that would focus on supporting quality of life for those living, working, and learning along the York Road corridor. Taking time to come together and listen to the community would be a critical part of this process. In 2009, Loyola executed a new strategic plan wherein it committed to taking a leadership role on York Road and engaging in "Listening Initiatives" with community members. "Without meaningful input," wrote Terry Sawyer, "this initiative will not be a success."

In the meantime, YRP began to consider how to leverage the SNAP, which contained well-vetted priorities for revitalization. Leaders knew that the planning charrettes and vetting process that created the SNAP had brought together hundreds of people. "We wanted to see if an effort to update the plan could be done in a way that would reinvigorate YRP, invite more people to participate, and force the city to focus anew on improving the corridor," Karen DeCamp explained.

Given the city's bureaucracy and limited resources, YRP recognized that volunteer efforts would need to be supplemented and began to consider bringing on an AmeriCorps VISTA member to organize a project that would convene groups of people and go to each community to update the SNAP.

In 2011, Karen received a $5,000 Bank of America Local Heroes Award for her work with YRP and donated it toward the cost share for an AmeriCorps VISTA. She issued a challenge to YRP membership, neighborhood associations, and York Road area stakeholders to raise enough funding to meet the additional cost of the position – about $11,000.

This VISTA was responsible for convening representatives from the York Road Partnership; individual neighborhood residents; Loyola University; Baltimore City government; local public schools; and faith, business, and nonprofit partners to update the SNAP with completed projects and updated recommendations that reflected the current situation. It was never meant to be a complete overhaul of the plan, rather a way to take stock of successes and update recommendations.

Underneath it all lay one of the most important goals of the VISTA's project and of Strong City's community organizing efforts: to build engagement and energy in YRP and to find and develop new people to incorporate into YRP, including the leadership and action committees.

Bolstered by positive collaboration with YRP as well as a sense that it needed to ensure the stability of the eastern edge of its Evergreen campus, Loyola University's York Road Initiative (YRI) was kicked off in 2010, led by Erin O'Keefe. Its mission was to collaborate with neighbors and partners to produce positive change for all residents in the York Road community: improving education and youth development, building civic capacity, and strengthening the York Road commercial corridor.

The YRI is a place-based community development strategy geographically focused in the Govans section of north Baltimore, specifically Cold Spring Lane (Loyola Evergreen Campus) to Northern Parkway (Loyola Clinical Centers at Belvedere Square). The Initiative intentionally involves community constituencies, including neighborhood residents and associations; faith-based, civic, and business organizations; and public and private leaders.

> Strong City had built a powerful relationship with Loyola University Maryland, one of Strong City's founding partners and among the most influential anchor institutions within YRP's footprint.

Where We Are and Where We're Going

Karen DeCamp's vision and expertise in coalition building took the structure of YRP that was set up in the late 1990s and early 2000s and built a large, diverse organization with a reputation for being tough but collaborative. Collective power was built from strong, positive relationships. This organization brings together people across race and income differences to get things done, and even has fun doing it.

When Karen became Director of Community Programs at Strong City, she was able to connect organizational resources with the work of community building – including the AmeriCorps VISTA program, the Community Schools program at Guilford Elementary/Middle and Govans Elementary, Strong City's fiscal sponsorship of YRP, and more.

The reinvigorated leadership within YRP laid the groundwork for the success of Loyola's YRI. After moving from Louisiana to the Winston-Govans neighborhood, Chris Forrest began attending neighborhood association meetings. A natural organizer and peacemaker, he spearheaded block projects and cleanup efforts and was asked to get more involved with YRP. In 2013, Chris was elected President of YRP, succeeding Eileen Gwin of Lake Walker (now deceased) and marking a shift for YRP toward centering black leadership in the corridor. (At this writing, Chris was still involved in YRP but had turned the reins of leadership over to Donna Blackwell.)

Under Chris Forrest's leadership, YRP continued to grow its committees, each of which sets yearly goals for its work. Chris worked with Loyola, City Councilman Bill Henry, and the Govanstowne Business Association to form the York Corridor Collective (YCC), a project focusing on improving the commercial corridor. With funding that Loyola applied for and won, the YCC brought the Urban Land Institute's team of experts to analyze the corridor, listen to local residents and business owners, and create a commercial vision plan. It's just one example of how, with dedicated staff support for the York Road Corridor, Loyola University had become "embedded in the neighborhood," said Erin

O'Keefe, YRI Director and former Strong City board member.

In collaboration with YRP, Loyola was able to save the DeWees Recreation Center after it was slated for closure, and to secure enough money to rehab the building and hire a full-time Community Recreation Council organizer. Loyola also worked closely with YRP to launch the Govanstowne Farmers' Market in 2011 to bring fresh food to the area. In recognition of those efforts and many others, the York Road Partnership named Loyola "Best Neighborhood Partner" in 2013.

Taking a page from our model in Barclay with Telesis, Strong City found funding to pair the Woodbourne-McCabe Habitat redevelopment with on-the-ground community building efforts. With the support of the Presbyterian churches that partnered with the Habitat project, Strong City hired a community organizer, Christian Hall, who from 2015 to 2019 worked to build stronger civic engagement and neighborhood leadership in east side neighborhoods of the York Road corridor. In early 2020, the churches were working with local community leaders to determine how to continue supporting Woodbourne-McCabe and other neighborhoods.

Meanwhile, the YRP's efforts to control troublesome liquor establishments had met with considerable success. Since starting this work, YRP as of late 2019 had eliminated five problem establishments, signed protective MOUs with five others, and stopped over a dozen attempts to locate new liquor licenses on the corridor.

With YRP widely seen as one of Baltimore's most effective neighborhood coalitions, Strong City began bringing lessons learned to its work around the city. Karen and Chris did a joint workshop presentation at Neighborhood Institute, Strong City's annual conference of community leaders and nonprofit professionals, in 2015 and 2016. In each case, they shared with about 40 participants key principles for working effectively across neighborhood boundaries.

The 2015 Uprising following the death of Freddie Gray revealed something about the power of engaged communities along York Road. The day after the unrest, a large group led by City Councilman Bill Henry gathered in the Loyola parking lot and made signs calling for peace and justice. Neighbors stood with the signs at the corner of York and Woodbourne, where people passing by joined them in a powerful statement of support and hope. Several miles south, Harwood and Barclay residents gathered along Greenmount Avenue with a similar purpose.

Karen DeCamp recalls: "Because we had relationships, because we had a way of communicating via social media and a huge listserv, we were able to get that message out. People pulled their cars over and joined us." That launched a tradition of annual peace walks to bring people together across York Road; in 2018, the peace walk was tied to the kickoff of one of the quarterly Baltimore Ceasefire anti-violence weekends.

The Uprising further underscored the need for YRP to center black communities and for allied institutions to do work "with, not for" those communities. In

2017, all YRP leaders underwent an Undoing Racism training sponsored by Loyola's Center for Community Service and Justice.

> With YRP widely seen as one of Baltimore's most effective neighborhood coalitions, Strong City began bringing lessons learned to its work around the city.

Key Strategies: York Road Partnership

Over the years, the York Road Partnership (YRP) leadership has encouraged people with energy to join committees or start new ones in line with agreed-upon priorities. These committees include:

1. **Housing and Neighborhood Revitalization.** This committee promotes a healthy and vibrant York Road community. It consists of neighborhood residents, government officials, community organizations, institutions, and other interested parties working collaboratively to strengthen neighborhood image, housing stock and desirability.

2. **Land Use and Problem Liquor Establishments.** YRP has a strong history of helping communities along the corridor deal with problem establishments, such as liquor stores

that are magnets for crime, loitering and trash. YRP has worked to reduce the number of liquor licenses in the corridor, learned to organize residents to challenge the city Liquor Board, and, with professional help, developed a Memorandum of Understanding for owners of new liquor establishments.

3. **Public Safety and Youth Development.** The main goal of this committee is to enhance the safety of the York Road community and, in turn, make it a more positive environment for youth. By working closely alongside residents, the Northern District Police, community centers, schools, and other partners, the committee addresses safety issues and promotes youth engagement. Strong City's longstanding partnership with the nearby Guilford Elementary School supported these efforts. This committee also successfully staged a number of public safety summits, each time attracting 50-100 residents who learn strategies for securing their communities and homes.

4. **Public Spaces and Greening.** This committee strives to enhance the York Road Corridor by ensuring the streetscape is attractive and green, and walkable and safe for pedestrians and cyclists. They advocate for and maintain public spaces on the Corridor and in neighborhoods, and work to ensure that bus services and fa-

cilities are available, accessible and convenient (including advocating for bus shelters).

York Road Partnership: Timeline/Fact Sheet

- In the 1990s, in the wake of neighborhood squabbles, Strong City is asked to moderate a community planning session on York Road
- In 1995, with encouragement from Strong City, the York Road Partnership (YRP) is formed to reach across the York Road race and class divide and tackle issues such as traffic, crime, drug dealing, and problem liquor stores
- Strong City holds a position on YRP's leadership committee, assists YRP with technical assistance, advice, and training
- In 2003, YRP is accepted into the city's Strategic Neighborhood Action Plan (SNAP) program; YRP's plan is accepted by the city in 2006
- In 2007, YRP leader Karen DeCamp joins Strong City to work on community and school strengthening; later, Karen continues to work closely on York Road issues as Strong City's Director of Community Programs
- In 2007, Strong City, following the model established in Barclay, connects Habitat for Humanity redevelopment work with community building efforts, hiring a community organizer with support of a group of Presbyte-

rian churches to build leadership east of York Road

- In 2009, Strong City persuades Loyola University Maryland, the largest local anchor institution, to become a more active player on York Road issues
- In 2011, Strong City assigns an AmeriCorps VISTA to work on York Road, charged with convening partners and updating the SNAP
- In 2011, Loyola kicks off its York Road Initiative, a place-based community development strategy, led by Erin O'Keefe, who serves on Strong City's Board for several years
- The YRP is fiscally sponsored by Strong City
- Strong City becomes the lead agency for Community Schools programs at Guilford Elementary/Middle and Govans Elementary schools
- At the close of the 2010s, the YRP, a mature organization with a more than 20-year track record, is widely regarded as one of the strongest, most diverse, and most effective neighborhood coalitions in the city

A York Road Partnership gathering prompted by the April 2015 death of Freddie Gray and the Baltimore Uprising launched a tradition of annual peace walks, bringing people together from east and west of York Road.

Strong City and the York Road Partnership identified the Woodbourne-McCabe neighborhood as a priority for blight removal. As of early 2020, Habitat for Humanity of the Chesapeake was transforming three blocks of McCabe Avenue into homes for low-income owners.

The York Road Partnership built a strong relationship with Loyola University Maryland. In the mid-2010s, Loyola received city and state funding to complete the "Bmore Birds" murals along York Road, in partnership with the YRP and the Govanstowne Business Association.

The Family Dollar store on York Road was welcomed as filling a community need when it arrived in 2005, but poor upkeep has been an ongoing problem. Residents, empowered through the York Road Partnership, have been vigilant in demanding accountability.

CONCLUSION/LESSONS

These accounts of Strong City's work with communities show what is possible. Meaningful change can happen even in places that outsiders dismiss as hopelessly devastated. Neighborhoods are complex, and a multi-pronged, place-based strategy is essential to address the key physical and social aspects of the community and build on existing assets and strengths. This model is founded upon key indicators based on our history of community organizing and neighborhood revitalization (as described in the Introduction and throughout this document). This is what we have learned over five decades of doing this work.

Lesson #1: Although neighborhood problems are unique and require context, their solutions are transferrable across communities.

The problems Baltimore faced in the 20th century and continues to face in the 21st are well known. The challenges of a post-industrial society combined with racist structures have created swaths of the city torn by extreme disinvestment, with areas of poverty trapped in cyclical losses of both economic capital and the "bridging" social capital that connects people in better-off areas to power and resources.

The neighborhoods in these case studies have suffered relatively similar problems to each other, and together they form a significant section of north-central Baltimore. Remington relied on mills, quarries, and factory jobs that disappeared. Barclay was severely affected by the manufacturing sector decline. All these neighborhoods suffered from the 1950s to 1980s from suburbanization and white flight, followed by middle-class black flight, along with the decline in available jobs and services, which created a massive vacant housing problem.

These vacant houses became dilapidated, which in turn increased disinvestment. The lack of jobs, and the high unemployment rates that followed, helped facilitate crime and drug epidemics that swept over neighborhoods and from which some are still recovering.

Perhaps the most telling connection these neighborhoods share is the demonstrable effect of policies and structures, often racially motivated, that disproportionately affected minority communities. Those policies left the neighborhoods of York Road divided along race and class lines and created a black unemployment rate double that of the national rate.

The impact of these issues is cumulative, as these problems do not exist in isolation but rather intersect and work to reinforce cyclical, generational poverty, disinvestment, lack of social capital, and systematic disenfranchisement. Understanding that these issues are connected is integral to working toward solutions. Strong City strategically utilized an intersecting set of programs and principles to effectively create change, support partner organizations, and, most importantly, strengthen communities and people.

The context for each of these challenges is unique, as it must be when examining neighborhoods with a location-specific methodology. However, this time-tested, successful model can work in other neighborhoods across Baltimore and beyond. It could readily apply to other cities, especially those that share the post-industrial problems that Baltimore faces: declining populations, structural racism, widespread disinvestment, and all the social ills that these elements promote.

> This time-tested, successful model can work in other neighborhoods across Baltimore and beyond. It could readily apply to other cities, especially those that share the post-industrial problems that Baltimore faces.

Lesson #2: Skilled community organizing is a critical tool for creating community change.

The presence of committed volunteers and enthusiastic residents is essential to transform a community, but experience teaches us that it is not sufficient. Trained, paid community organizing is also indispensable to catalyze change that harnesses community assets – most importantly, the gifts, knowledge, and passion of residents. Without on-the-ground organizing that connects directly and deeply with community members, efforts to address the persistent problems neighborhoods face are likely to lack community buy-in and ultimately to fail.

Throughout Strong City's decades of work, we have found that before formal programs can take off, community organizing and building up communal support are essential to effectively implement, and plan, program design. We saw this in the classrooms of Harwood and on the streets of Remington. The most vivid example may be the Barclay neighborhood, where the work of VISTA members spurred creation of the Barclay Leadership Council (BLC), which in turn laid the groundwork for the Barclay Midway Old Goucher Coalition (BMOG) – with Strong City organizers playing a supporting role every step of the way. Strong City's successful initiatives along the York Road Corridor further demonstrate the key role skilled organizing plays in building community engagement and neighborhood leadership.

That level of community support is maintained by Strong City's ongoing commitment to the communities where we work. Sometimes our involvement comes to a natural end, as in Remington, where Strong City is no longer needed thanks to the emergence of a mature, effective association of residents and the creation of a robust neighborhood plan. But in other neighborhoods, the impact of our organizing is reinforced and extended through, for example, our operation of the 29th Street Community Center, our presence in individual schools stretching over many years, and our commitment to keeping the doors open at The Club at Collington Square, a vital afterschool program in our new neighborhood in East Baltimore. Different circumstances in different places call for different responses.

Lesson #3: Impact is strongest when it is created collectively and planned by the community itself, not imposed from outside.

Strong City believes that true change happens when neighborhood residents are integrally involved. To handle large-scale projects that transform communities, those communities must have an association or neighborhood alliance that is able to negotiate on equal footing with outside partners, while speaking on behalf of community members. Along with cultivating local leadership, Strong City has often helped to run projects led by residents or done in partnership with the community to create a more cohesive network of residents, thereby increasing community support.

The success of the Barclay Telesis development exemplifies this approach, as through the entire development process, the BMOG Coalition that represents the residents negotiated with Telesis Corp. to ensure community needs were met. Remington also serves as a clear example of the importance of robust, grassroots leadership and planning by consensus, as formation of the Greater Remington Improvement Association (GRIA) was essential to that community's progress.

The York Road Partnership (YRP) and all the good work that flowed from its formation were only possible after a group of neighborhoods and businesses invited

Strong City to intervene and moderate their collaborative process. This followed years of infighting and failed partnerships along the corridor among disparate neighborhoods. By 2007, the YRP was one of the strongest, most diverse associations in the city.

Perhaps most striking is how Harwood was able to respond effectively to a spike in violence. Before our community building efforts were fully launched in 2005, the community association struggled to maintain relevancy as residents feared getting involved after the association president's home was firebombed. But after a rash of shootings in 2012, neighborhood leaders stood together and began a series of weekly block leader trainings and monthly Neighborhood Leaders Forums. The residents found that collectively they were much stronger than when it was one person shouldering the responsibility of the neighborhood.

In each of these cases, organizers helped by identifying and encouraging neighborhood residents with leadership potential, and by guiding those emerging leaders to learn and grow, become problem solvers, and gain access to new knowledge and resources. Once strong neighborhood leadership is in place, the organizer steps back, putting the spotlight where it belongs: on residents assuming leadership in their own communities.

> Once strong neighborhood leadership is in place, the organizer steps back, putting the spotlight where it belongs: on residents assuming leadership in their own communities.

Lesson #4: In doing this work, do not attempt to be "colorblind."

Racism, in particular anti-black racism, is America's original sin. The consequences of slavery, legal and de facto segregation, and institutional racism are a daily fact of life in Baltimore and most other American cities. The precise contours of this issue vary from place to place; Baltimore, a majority African-American city where the nation's first official housing segregation ordinance was written, grapples with a different legacy than, say, Los Angeles, a multilingual, multiethnic mixing bowl where Hispanic people are the majority. But racism has pervaded America since well before its founding, and a clear-eyed recognition of this fact must inform all efforts at neighborhood-based work.

Karen DeCamp of the YRP recognized this reality when she made the explicit decision to "name the divide" separating the mostly white and affluent areas from the mostly black and lower-income areas on either side of York Road. White-led organizations and white organizers in particular must engage in ongoing education and reflection about the scourge of white supremacy on communities – and their own role in perpetuating it. They should realize that however good their intentions are, misunderstandings and hurt feelings are at times unavoidable, and they need to learn from their mistakes and always seek to do better.

At the same time, it should be recognized that good organizing, supported and sustained over time, is one way we can begin to bridge the racial and class divides that tear at urban communities. As in the case of the YRP, skilled organizers have a role to play in knitting together adjacent neighborhoods that may look very different, and begin to change the dynamics of how resource allocation has been dictated by structurally racist policies.

Lesson #5: Physical, tangible improvements, even small ones, are crucial to a neighborhood turnaround.

Capital improvements can drastically change the aesthetics of the neighborhood, as well as increasing the likelihood of future investments. Many of these initiatives, such as community gardens and murals, are not typical "development" projects, but they build civic identity by making people feel good about where they live. This key but difficult-to-define aspect of community building is essential to create before large-scale projects can begin, as those major efforts require community buy-in and support.

The effect of physical improvements is cumulative, eventually transforming a troubled neighborhood into a strong one. We believe that these tangible improvements must take place alongside community building efforts. Strong City works with Healthy Neighborhoods, which brings in capital to improve the physical condition of neighborhoods, and we partner with the city Housing Department's Code Enforcement Section to tackle the blight that gnaws at neighborhoods from the inside out.

In Remington, Strong City worked with residents to instigate street and sidewalk repairs; improve lighting and cleanliness; reduce blight; and complete other streetscape enhancements. Residents also worked together to remove rat infestations, fix sewage issues, improve trash pickup, and renew the local park to keep their neighborhood clean and green. Strong City-trained block leaders oversaw more than 30 Healthy Neighborhoods block projects.

This work culminated in raising median home prices, thereby building community wealth for legacy residents. It also attracted new capital from the Mayor's Office of Neighborhoods and the Department of Planning, which worked with GRIA to recruit new businesses and develop large-scale projects. One result of these efforts was the very popular and successful R. House development.

A more anecdotal story that reflects the importance of improving the "feel" of a neighborhood comes from Harwood, where Strong City encouraged residents to enter the Charles Village Painted Ladies Contest, and all 10 families that participated won first place in Healthy Neighborhoods Initiatives.

Strong City's housing programs have transformed vacant homes into opportunities for low- and middle-income owners along York Road and in Harwood, drastically altering public perceptions of those communities. In Barclay, a neighborhood once labeled as among Baltimore's most disinvested ended the decade of the 2010s with hundreds of affordable new homes and fewer than 100 vacants.

Through Strong City's collaborative efforts with many partners, we have seen the vacant property rate reduced by over 50 percent in our targeted neighborhoods, spurring millions of dollars in investment and demonstrating a replicable model for Baltimore and beyond. This is one of our proudest accomplishments.

Lesson #6: Change takes time and persistence – there are no quick fixes

The problems affecting Remington, Harwood, Barclay, and York Road were built up over decades. The changes that Strong City helped foster in these neighborhoods happened slowly, often incrementally. The lesson here is that it generally takes at least a full decade, once ground-level organizing has begun, for a neighborhood in decline to show comprehensive and sustainable improvements. However, capturing the full development arc of a disinvested community can take far longer.

This work requires patience, and those who are serious about it must commit to being involved for the long haul. The Barclay-Telesis project essentially began in 2003, when the Barclay Midway Old Goucher

Coalition (BMOG) was created in preparation for the upcoming redevelopment scheduled by the city; Telesis finally broke ground in 2010. The YRP applied, and was later accepted, for the Strategic Neighborhood Action Plan in 2003. Their official plan was given to the city in 2004, but it was not implemented until 2006, and was updated with the help of a VISTA in 2011. Remington began working on its neighborhood plan in 2008; the City finally approved the plan in 2018.

Strong City's involvement in a neighborhood may last years or decades, but even when the work is "over," it never truly ends. Strengthening neighborhoods and residents is an ongoing commitment with no expiration date. When Strong City moves on from a neighborhood, as in the case of Remington, we know that others – often with the skills and training Strong City helped to provide – will continue where we left off. Indeed, one purpose of our annual Neighborhood Institute conference for community leaders, launched in 2007, is to continue supporting places where we have worked in the past but are no longer involved on a daily basis.

After decades of disinvestment and its attendant problems, Barclay, Harwood, Remington, and the York Road Corridor have emerged as strong, stable places. Together, a dynamic mix of legacy residents and more recent arrivals lead the charge to improve their neighborhoods. These communities reflect the passion, determination, and perseverance of the residents Strong City has worked side-by-side with since 1969.

The revival of these places counters a pernicious, deficit-oriented narrative that paints the problems of urban America – and, in recent years, Baltimore in particular – as intractable, even hopeless. Like cities across America and the world, Baltimore has serious challenges, but solutions are available to those who know what to do, and are willing and able to do the work.

> After decades of disinvestment and its attendant problems, Barclay, Harwood, Remington, and the York Road Corridor have emerged as strong, stable places. Together, a dynamic mix of legacy residents and more recent arrivals lead the charge to improve their neighborhoods.

NOTES

i.   http://www.worc.org/media/Howto-Understand-Role-of-Community-Organizer.pdf

ii.   http://www.worc.org/media/Howto-Understand-Role-of-Community-Organizer.pdf

iii.   https://news.google.com/newspapers?nid=2205&-dat=19990521&id=epslAAAAIBAJ&sjid=xvQ-FAAAAIBAJ&pg=4420,5210071&hl=en

iv.   http://www.cphabaltimore.org/ferebee/

v.   http://www.parksandpeople.org/files/resources/2577_Vacant%20Lot%20Restoration%20Program%20Report.pdf

vi.   http://www.urban.org/sites/default/files/alfresco/publication-pdfs/411866-Systems-to-Improve-the-Management-of-City-Owned-Land-in-Baltimore.PDF

vii.   http://www.centralbaltimore.org/uncategorized/peoples-homesteading-group-receives-2015-dennis-livingston-creativity-perseverance-award/

viii.   http://articles.baltimoresun.com/2004-01-17/news/0401170051_1_project-5000-property-city-plans

ix.   http://articles.baltimoresun.com/2013-01-18/news/bs-md-ci-kelly-column-barclay-20130118_1_barclay-street-neighborhood-house-greenmount-avenue

x.   http://www.baltimoresun.com/news/maryland/bal-te.md.harwood19sep19-story.html

xi.   https://en.wikipedia.org/wiki/Remington, Baltimore

xii.   Remington Neighborhood Plan, p. 17

xiii.   Remington Neighborhood Plan, p. 18

xiv.   Remington Neighborhood Fact Book, p. 6

xv.   Live Baltimore

xvi.   Johns Hopkins University Remington Engagement Initiative, p. 4

xvii.   http://www.griaonline.org/neighborhood-plan/

xviii.   2010 Census

xix.   http://www.baltimoresun.com/ph-ms-seawall-0920-20120918-story.html

xx.   http://www.bizjournals.com/baltimore/blog/real-estate/2015/08/proposed-remington-zoning-changes-give-hope-to.html

xxi.   Bednar, Adam, "Neighbors oppose liquor store presence," The Baltimore Messenger, Week of December 27, 2007

Apprentice
House Press
Loyola University Maryland

Apprentice House is the country's only campus-based, student-staffed book publishing company. Directed by professors and industry professionals, it is a nonprofit activity of the Communication Department at Loyola University Maryland.

Using state-of-the-art technology and an experiential learning model of education, Apprentice House publishes books in untraditional ways. This dual responsibility as publishers and educators creates an unprecedented collaborative environment among faculty and students, while teaching tomorrow's editors, designers, and marketers.

Outside of class, progress on book projects is carried forth by the AH Book Publishing Club, a co-curricular campus organization supported by Loyola University Maryland's Office of Student Activities.

Eclectic and provocative, Apprentice House titles intend to entertain as well as spark dialogue on a variety of topics. Financial contributions to sustain the press's work are welcomed. Contributions are tax deductible to the fullest extent allowed by the IRS.

To learn more about Apprentice House books or to obtain submission guidelines, please visit www.apprenticehouse.com.

Apprentice House
Communication Department
Loyola University Maryland
4501 N. Charles Street
Baltimore, MD 21210
Ph: 410-617-5265
info@apprenticehouse.com • www.apprenticehouse.com